from A. C. ~September 2007

SITTING STRONG: WRESTLING WITH THE ORNERY GOD

1 cor. 10:10

Smyth & Helwys Publishing, Inc.
6316 Peake Road
Macon, Georgia 31210-3960
1-800-747-3016
©2006 by Smyth & Helwys Publishing
All rights reserved.
Printed in the United States of America.

The paper used in this publication meets the minimum requirements of
American National Standard for Information Sciences—
Permanence of Paper for Printed Library Materials.
ANSI Z39.48–1984. (alk. paper)

Library of Congress Cataloging-in-Publication Data

Miley, Jeanie.
Sitting strong : wrestling with the ornery God / by Jeanie Miley.
p. cm.
ISBN 1-57312-470-2 (pbk. : alk. paper)
1. Suffering—Religious aspects—Christianity.
2. Consolation
I. Title.

BV4909.M49 2006
248.8'6—dc21

2006011553

Other titles by Jeanie Miley:
Ancient Psalms for Contemporary Pilgrims
Becoming Fire: Experiencing the Presence of Jesus Every Day
Christheart: A Way of Knowing Jesus
The Spiritual Art of Creative Silence: Lessons in Christian Meditation

SITTING STRONG

WRESTLING WITH THE ORNERY GOD

BY JEANIE MILEY

To the memory of
Sherry Holmes
and for
Erin and Allison

With deepest appreciation and love for my fellow travelers
in the Thursday Morning Bible Study
at River Oaks Baptist Church
and the
Monday Night Bible Study
St. Luke's United Methodist Church
and
for all who have allowed me
into your sacred spaces of suffering
and for all who have been with me in mine

Table of Contents

Tribute

Despair is presumptuous.
—JOHN ROWAN CLAYPOOL

I first read John Claypool's classic book *Tracks of a Fellow Struggler* in 1971. Earlier that year, the birth of our first child had been accompanied by a terrible scare. I had read John's account of the death of his own daughter with a mixture of gratitude and terror in the face of the danger and fragility of life. John's unique confessional writing helped me face my own fears.

Later that summer, John was the speaker at Student Week in Glorieta, New Mexico, and my husband and I invited him to be our guest for Mexican food in Santa Fe.

I'll never forget that John insisted that I sit in the front seat with my husband while he took the back seat.

As we traveled into Santa Fe, I said to John, "I know that this is so little to say in the face of your loss, but I have to tell you how much your work, your book, and your messages this week have meant to me. I have to say thank you."

"That you have found meaning in my loss somehow takes some of the absurdity out of the experience," he said quietly. Always gracious, John taught me a most important lesson: that it is acceptable to admit the reality and the feelings of absurdity of our deepest losses, and that there is meaning in those things we cannot bear. He also taught me that our suffering, carried consciously and in the mercy of God, can light the way in others' darkness.

Throughout these decades, John's teaching in that moment, in subsequent encounters, and through his magnificent writing and preaching have shaped my understanding of life and of suffering.

It was John Claypool who taught me first that, as he was fond of saying, "Life is gift." John also taught all of us who listened to him and loved him that the gift contains both joy and sorrow. It was John who first showed how the wounds we think will destroy us can give hope to someone else.

John had graciously agreed to write the foreword to this book.

Instead, I write this tribute to him in the week following his death on September 3, 2005.

He was a light to those of us who were privileged to know him. He was a way-shower, a gentle guide, a comforter, a giver of grace, a lover of people and life, and a friend of God.

Introduction

*"I am convinced that the way we deal with pain
is the acid test of our faith."*
—Daniel Vestal

On a breathtakingly beautiful summer morning, I rushed from the parking lot into the retreat center of St. Benedict's Monastery in Snowmass, Colorado. I was rushing because I had wavered between going for the early morning "sit" in the meditation room and staying in my room. Afraid of being flooded with grief in that holy stillness, I had held back, but at the last minute I thought that, perhaps, the power of opening my mind and heart to God in the presence of other seekers might be healing.

Across the parking lot, I saw Brother Charlie, one of the monks who had been such a gracious presence in my previous retreats at the monastery. Clothed in jeans and a work shirt, he was hauling trash to the dumpster at the retreat center.

I hadn't seen him since I had arrived, so I eagerly started toward him, forgetting the rule of silence and spontaneously calling out his name.

"Don't come near me," he said. "I've been hauling trash and I'm a mess." And then his whole expression changed, as if he could sense my turmoil.

"How are you?" he asked quietly. My eyes filled with tears, and I said, "Not so good, Charlie. I almost didn't come for the sit this morning."

"Sit strong, Jeanie. *Sit strong!*" he said, and I sucked in my breath. I could remember my father's saying to me any time I was in a hard spot, "Sit steady in the boat, Jeanie. Sit steady in the boat."

You just never know when a trash heap is going to become holy ground.

Charlie's words that morning echoed in my heart during every one of the prayer periods of that retreat. I knew I could not *be strong*, but the intention to *sit strong*—to endure the pain I was experiencing and not run away from it, to accept it as part of my process, to go into it instead of running away from it—was precisely what I needed to do.

Indeed, sitting strong was, for me, about letting myself be weak and tired and scared. It was about allowing myself to feel all the feelings I'd not allowed myself to feel in my busy life. Sitting strong was holding that intention of being with God, even in my suffering and especially with my suffering, allowing the Divine Therapist to comfort and console me.

Sitting strong and consenting to the inner work of that Divine Therapist was my assignment in the gritty, grueling process that Thomas Keating calls "the unloading of the unconscious" and the challenge to the emotional programming of a lifetime.

For eleven days, I took my many selves, those flawed and fragmented parts of myself, to the meditation hall for each "sit." Each time, I expressed my intention to *sit strong* in the presence of God, holding my hopes and my hurts before that Presence.

Within a few weeks, I was back in Houston, Texas, teaching my Thursday morning Bible study. For that year, the study was the book of Job.

How could I have known when we chose the book of Job that our first class would be in the same week as the horrific events of September 11?

How could we have known that this would be the last year of Sherry Holmes' life, the year that she would suffer through the final days of cancer?

Sherry had been one of the most faithful members of my Thursday morning Bible study at River Oaks Baptist Church, but in the year that I taught Job her presence was a silent and beautiful reminder of what it means to *sit strong*.

Every week, as I gathered my commentaries and my Bible and prepared the lecture and the questions for the week's study, it was as if Sherry came and sat with me at my desk. Every thought that I had, every question I formulated, every word that I would speak was filtered through the questions, "How will Sherry hear this?" and "How will this sound to Sherry's young daughters and her husband as they stand with their mother and wife through this suffering?"

Looking back on that year, I now know that Sherry was silently giving me more than I ever gave to her, and I will forever be grateful for the gift of her presence, her friendship, and her silent witness to the power of *sitting strong* in the midst of the unthinkable and the unbearable. Indeed, Sherry modeled grace in incomparable ways; she suffered her fate with such dignity that all of us who were touched by her were transformed by her life to one degree or another.

Sherry *sat strong* that year. She carried her suffering with a beauty, dignity, and uncommon composure, showing us all how to face the unthinkable. In the presence of her friends and family, and those who barely knew her, Sherry lived out what would become, for me, the theme of this book.

This book isn't about the meaning of suffering. It isn't about the process of grief or the way to get through the difficulties of life, and it makes no promises about what you will gain by reading it. There are no easy steps through suffering.

Instead, *Sitting Strong* suggests that when life knocks the props out from under you and you are stunned with the pain of it all, it is possible to gather up your agony and sit with it in the presence of God, who may, admittedly, feel either absent or like the enemy at the moment. This book is not about *being strong*; instead, it is about that terrible time when all you can do is stumble onto the ash heap of suffering, as Job did, and simply sit with your suffering, wrestling with it, arguing with God, and letting the old die so that the new can be born.

Throughout years of studying and teaching the book of Job, I have come to identify certain experiences as "Job experiences." Unlike daily annoyances or irritations, a Job experience throws you to the mat, leaving you stunned and disoriented, dismayed and grief-stricken, humiliated and stripped of your ordinary ways of dealing with life and your comfortable, protective, well-worn defenses.

A Job experience can occur from out of the blue, like a sudden tragedy, or it can come to your consciousness slowly, over time. A Job experience is one in which all of the answers that have worked for you in the past no longer work and you are forced to face yourself and your life in a new way. It can be brought on by the choices of other people or by a chance or quirk of nature. Sometimes we make the choices that take us to the mat of our own failures, and there is a peculiar agony about falling from grace in your own eyes and by your own hand.

Indeed, life is often most unfair. It is difficult, hard, messy, and sometimes almost intolerable, and no one escapes its ravages. *Sitting Strong* suggests that walking into your difficulty and sitting with it has the potential of transforming you.

A Job experience leaves you changed, and the hard truth is that while some people are refined and made more compassionate and wise through their Job experience, others become bitter or vindictive. Some people are transformed by what happens to them, but others begin to die, cell by cell, by the tragedies that have struck them.

Sitting Strong suggests that no matter how weak you feel or actually are, it is possible that the very pain that you think will destroy you can, if you will hold it in consciousness and work it, be an instrument of healing.

Sitting Strong is an invitation to weaken into our losses and lean into our pain in such a way that we are changed. It is about the process of allowing the pain that we have experienced to wake us up to ourselves. It is about letting the pain be the teacher and the guide. It is about holding the pain in consciousness long enough to understand it. It is about the long, hard, tedious, perilous, and sometimes unbearable process of conversion, transformation, redemption, and salvation. It is, I trust, a book about authentic and radical hope.

I believe that in the darkest suffering, God is present, attempting to heal, transform, liberate, and empower persons. In choosing not to waste our sorrows, God's redemptive work is free to work.

I believe and affirm that no matter how hard the challenge or excruciating the pain, there are golden threads of God's redeeming love woven into our sorrows and our losses, our failures and our crises, our character defects and our agony.

God, who is infinitely creative and resourceful, is at work in all things, attempting to bring about good. That is, I believe, the foundation of good theology. Our task is to find where it is that God is at work and then cooperate with that creative, redemptive energy of the One-Who-Makes-All-Things-New.

Sitting Strong is a way to help God help us.

I cannot guarantee that you will find the answers you want by reading this book. I do not know if you will find the reason for your own personal pain or the meaning or purpose in it. I cannot promise that you will "feel better" if you read it. I hope, however, that you will know yourself and God better and that you will experience the presence of God in the midst of your own suffering. My prayer is that you will come to know God as both Comforter and Disturber, the One who makes all things new.

Oh, God—you are sometimes an ornery God—
　　　you take me down roads I'd never planned to travel.
You expose me to
stuff that I thought
I'd never have to
look at, much less handle.
　　　　You travel me too fast into places I don't know how to
navigate or negotiate . . .
and you leave me stuck
too long in messy places I cannot
bear . . .
　　　　　and then you ask me to trust you!
　　　And so I scream,　　　*Who do you think you are to mess with
　　　　　　　　　　me like this?*

Oh, God, you are a troublesome God . . . and sometimes
I think your absence seems easier
than the white-hot heat of your disturbing, disrupting,
disorienting
presence.
　　　　Sometimes I keep getting the feeling
　　　　　that while I thought you were an orderly, dignified God,
most at home in the temple
and the church, the mosque
or the ivory tower, all high and holy and
lifted up above the ragged edges of my tattered, frazzled world,
　　　　you are, instead, most at home, hiding out in the broken
places,
　　　　the messy places . . . those very places I don't want to go.

I'm beginning to suspect that you are, after all, right in the middle of
my
　　pain.
　　　You are right in the middle of my character defect.
　　　You are in my doubts, my confusions, my questions.
　　　You are in my brokenness, my woundedness, my emptiness.
　　　There you are, right in the middle of the thing that I think I
　　　　cannot bear.
And you are there, Holy Presence, in what feels like absence.

Oh, Holy Autonomy . . . Constant, Pursuing Grace,
  your light is in the darkest night, your song in the deepest
        silence.

Grant me the grace to see
you
where you are
and as you are.

Grant me the grace to see and hear and
feel and taste and know . . . and receive . . .
your ornery love that never lets me go.

Life Happens

*It isn't that bad things happen to good people that bothers me. I've
pretty well made peace with that. It's that good things happen to bad*
people! But, then, who are the good people and who are the bad ones?

—JEANIE MILEY

"So, what did you expect God to do for you?"

The question, gently asked, came through the space between us and
walloped me in the face of my well-polished defenses.

The adult part of me gave some kind of sensible, theologically sound,
grown-up answer, but the kid in me was kicking and screaming: *I expected
more of God than this!—after all I've done for him!*

Sitting upright, like a lady, I wanted to double over in pain and protest
against the plight I was in. Internally, I railed again my fate. My pain was
almost unbearable, and I could not make it go away. Surely, I deserved better
than this! I've been a good person. I was a good little girl. I followed the rules
. . . and I expected God to take better care of me than this!

Now, of course, I didn't admit those childish responses aloud, and the
truth is that they surprised even me. I would have *died* before I would have
admitted them to anyone else, but I could not escape the fact that they were
roaring in my head. I felt as if I were a two-year-old, stomping and kicking,
flailing my arms, and pitching a fit. All the time, I was actually sitting calmly,
as if I really were an adult.

I was beyond the typical protest questions when life happens, such as "Why me? Why this? Why now?" I was facing God-as-I-used-to-know-him and myself, as I never wanted to be, demanding, *Why didn't you stop this! I was counting on you not to let this happen!*

Somehow, the child in me still believed that if I were good, God would protect me and bless me; if not, he would punish me. As much as I hate to admit it, I'd spent my life trying to be good enough to get the blessings and work hard enough to avoid the problems.

That God will take care of his special children, those of us who follow the rules and do the right things, is the grand seduction of the religious world in which I grew up. I don't know that anyone ever actually told me that if I obeyed God's laws and performed good deeds, I would be exempt from the suffering that the bad guys brought upon themselves. Somehow, I expected some kind of special protection or perhaps a holy insulation from the ordinary vicissitudes of *being human*.

I am embarrassed to admit it, and I can't really imagine any Sunday school classes in which it was overtly said that the religious life was based on a reward and punishment system. Somehow, the great lies about life with God seeped into my mind, leading me to expect special favors from God, or at least protection from the horrors of life, if I would only *believe right*, follow the rules, be nice, and give my tithe to the church.

In the midst of my adult crisis of faith, I would not have told anyone that I was still operating out of that childish misbelief about God and suffering, but the truth was that while I could spout a backpack full of platitudes about God, when I was slammed with four hard crises all at once, I was introduced in a hurry to that grand seduction that no less a man than the biblical giant Job faced in himself.

*

What was it that brought Job to the place where God could begin the tedious work of redemption in him? And why is it that, throughout the centuries, generations of people have turned to the book of Job to find their way through their own suffering? Why does Job's story have such staying power?

Job was, according to the sacred story, a "righteous man." He followed all the rules. He offered sacrifices, even on behalf of his children, apparently hoping to build a hedge of protection high enough to prevent them from suffering. He was successful in the eyes of others, admired and respected, and then, in short order, Job lost everything that he had counted on to give him meaning and purpose in life. Shattered and stripped of everything, including, finally, his health, he could do nothing but take himself to the ash heap and sit in anguished silence with his agony as his companion.

Job is, for us, not so much a model of patience, but a way-shower to wholeness, for in his suffering Job retreated to the ash heap and sat with his agony until he was transformed by the work of God, who took that very pain and agony that could have killed Job and used the raw materials of his grief to redeem Job.

During that long sit on the ash heap, Job wrestled with himself and his own life's story. Surely, Job must have gone back over his life and made a thorough examination of his choices in an attempt to understand how he had wound up where he was.

Second, Job wrestled with his friends, and it is those "friends" who can represent for us either our own inner voices or particular people in our world who are stunned by what happens to us.

Finally, Job wrestled with God, and neither of them let go until, out of the suffering, came the transformation. God worked in the midst of what was irreparable to restore and re-create Job, and for those of us who find ourselves forced to sit with that which we think we cannot bear, Job is a beacon of hope.

The ash heap, then, stands as a metaphor for us. It is not necessarily a place where we go, although it could be, so much as it is the process of suffering consciously what has happened to us in order to find the meaning in it. It represents the time we spend integrating our sorrows, coming to terms with what has happened to us or what we have lost. In *sitting strong*, we take seriously our grieving, honoring it by going into our pain with awareness.

It is Job who shows us that God is at work in all things, attempting to bring about good. It is Job who shows us that if we will wait on God, God will, finally, act, but sometimes God takes a very long time.

God is, I've heard, never late, but God often misses opportunities to be early.

What kinds of things bring us to the point of being open and available for God to move deeply into our agony and begin to heal us and transform us? What does it mean to suffer, and what does it mean to "sit with your pain"? This book intends to explore those questions, but first it is necessary to differentiate between Job experiences and other kinds of problems.

*

On a cold Valentine's Day, I sat at one of Houston's busiest intersections with my husband, facing north.

It was rush hour, and a man in a large sedan, going west on San Felipe, began furiously honking his horn at the woman in front of him, who was waiting to turn south onto Willowick. Apparently, he didn't realize that the restriction against turning left at that intersection had been lifted, and in his red-faced frustration, he increased his honking, lowered his car window, and began yelling and gesturing at the woman who was doing nothing but trying to turn left.

I could imagine him telling his wife, "You won't believe what happened to me today!" As angry as he was, he could have used that irritation as an excuse to drink all night. Maybe he took his anger out on his wife, which she could have then taken out on her neighbor or their children. Possibly his blood pressure shot up, and the woman in the car may have had an upset stomach. Sometimes people get mad enough over the smallest things and . . . well, they die!

Now, the woman hadn't set out to irritate the man. She wasn't doing anything illegal, unethical, or wrong. She was probably simply going home from work, leaving her cleaning, or picking up her children from school, but she inadvertently put that man in the sedan into a red zone of rage.

As we threaded our way through the dense traffic, I recalled the words on a baby bib I'd seen while shopping for my new granddaughter. In big, red letters the bib pronounced the universal truth, "Spit Happens!"

Indeed, daily life is fraught with difficulty and inconvenience, disaster and danger, and it takes a degree of consciousness to tell the difference between what is an irritation and what is a real problem. Surely, maturity demands of us that we learn to differentiate between and among the serious and the trivial and not shoot cannons at mosquitoes.

Later, as I was griping about the fact that my laptop was broken and my desktop computer was so outdated that I could not receive vital information from my editors, someone said to me, "You must feel like Job!"

Stunned, I responded quickly, "Oh, no. Computer problems do not qualify as a *Job experience!*"

Prior to 9/11, we already lived in a thick soup of anxiety-producing stimuli in our daily lives, but given the changes in our culture since the tragedy of September 11, anxiety and stress have been amped up to excruciating decibels. As horrible as the tragedy of 9/11 was, however, an even greater tragedy could be the incapacitating effects of living in a constant state of "terror alert" and the annihilation of hope.

Adults must learn to live in a world where bad things happen to good people not just now and then, but rather routinely. It is essential for mature and responsible people to be able to negotiate the shark-infested waters of everyday life where all of the best medical help in the world is sometimes not enough and all of the best financial strategies come to naught. We have to do more than just survive when our children don't conform to our expectations, when our marriages fail, and when we don't have what we want when we want it. We can and we must learn to be resilient people, people who are able to thrive, even in the midst of imperfection, incompletion, insufficiency, loss, and even *suffering*.

"If you fall apart when the toast burns," the old adage asks, "what will you do when your house burns?"

The truth is that we must learn to distinguish between real difficulties and minor irritations. We can learn to conserve our energy so that we do not waste it on the small stuff and so that when we come to the big stuff we are not all used up.

We need to learn the difference between an authentic tragedy and a bump in the road that you can get over.

We must examine the difference between those things that we have brought on ourselves, either by neglect, ignorance, or willful disregard and defiance, and those things that others bring into our lives. We must come to terms with the fact that some things are random acts of nature, and other stuff is the baggage we have inherited.

There is a difference in the way you respond to an acute or immediate crisis and the way you handle an ongoing, chronic condition, and we can learn the life skills necessary for responding to either. It really is possible to learn the difference between the things you cannot change and the things you can, and must, change.

It takes time, sometimes, to discover the difference between those things you can change or solve and the things that will require you to let go and let someone else handle. And, sometimes, we must face that *one thing* that requires us to change our entire lifestyle for the rest of our lives.

Working with the various things that happen in people's lives, it is clear to me that a Job experience falls into one of two categories: "The Sudden Blitz" or "The Thorn in the Flesh."

(1) *The Sudden Blitz:* A sudden catastrophe or loss, one of life's great tragedies that crashes into your life without warning, stripping from you something that is precious, qualifies as a Job experience. The loss of a child, the untimely death of a spouse or a significant other, the failure of a marriage or a lifelong dream, financial disaster, a catastrophic illness, a violent act of nature, or the violent act of one human being against himself or another person all qualify as Job experiences.

(2) *The Thorn in the Flesh:* The thorn in the flesh is that condition which is longstanding. It could be a character defect, a health issue, an addiction, a chronic pain or wounding from childhood that you will deal with the rest of your life. It could be a troublesome relationship that has shaped your life, an abandonment or rejection by a parent, an ongoing family dynamic that sucks life and energy from you, or a life script from your family of origin that has burdened you or broken you. Perhaps you made a choice in adolescence that you have had to "pay for" for all of your life; perhaps you are the carrier of your family's secret or shame. Whatever it is, it finally comes roaring to the surface, demanding to be acknowledged, healed, or forgiven.

Another Job experience with a uniquely difficult twist is the pain you have caused another person, whether by accident, carelessness, neglect, or outright defiance. Being able to recognize, admit, and accept what you have done that has injured someone else, and then doing whatever you can, as you can and when you can, to make amends or restitution is a way of cooperating with the redemptive mercy and grace of God.

Living with the pain of harming another person can be unbearable, except for the grace of God, which allows us to experience that recognition and then to do something about it. One who can walk into the wounds that he has inflicted on another person, including himself, can experience radical healing.

Whatever has happened to you, you can know that it is a Job experience when there is nothing you can do to change it or make it go away. You aren't rich enough, well connected enough, smart or clever enough, powerful or well-educated enough to change the problem, and one way or another, this problem is going to be with you. It is yours, and you must face it.

You will know it is a Job experience when you fel as if you cannot bear the pain, when you feel that you cannot go on, when you feel that the pain is going to devour you. You will know it is a Job experience when it feels that God is silent and all you can do is pray, "Help me!"

*

When I was a child, my father was pastor of First Baptist Church in Greenville, Texas, where he met every Monday morning with a group of fellow pastors, one of whom was uncommonly joyful and optimistic.

"What is your secret?" the other ministers asked him on a dreary day when they were experiencing that letdown common to ministers after Sunday.

"Ah, my secret?" he asked, smiling. "I believe the Good Book when it says that things have *come to pass*. My troubles, they don't come to stay. They come to pass."

Well, yes, sometimes.

Job teaches us how to behave when we are faced with the opposite of that truth. Some of our troubles come and take up residence in our lives, shaping us forever, and how we learn to live with those kinds of things determines everything about the quality of our lives. How we learn to survive with that thing we cannot change, that wound that will not heal, that blow that forever changes the landscape of our lives is all in learning how to sit with it long enough to integrate it into our lives in a healthy and creative way.

And that's not that easy when you're hurting.

*

I'm pretty much an expert on what doesn't work when life knocks you to your face. I can speak with fairly significant authority on the power of denial and refusing to see the problem and own the problem. I can describe multiple ways of pushing things under the carpet, avoiding conflict, and pretending that something doesn't exist. I can even tell the truth, now, about how easy it is to massage the truth and manage the distortions to keep from telling the truth.

It is possible to live for a very long time with "a secret" that you don't want anyone to know, especially you. Now and then, the entire energy of a family or a person is committed to keeping the family secret; ultimately, however, those things you don't want to know come out into the open.

People often blame or attack others for the pain in their own lives; in fact, we humans do inflict pain on each other, and we often inflict it onto the people we say we love most or the ones who are closest to us. In truth, however, blame and attack only exacerbate the pain. Children blame, I've found, and adults take responsibility.

Sometimes a big hurt of childhood lies festering for decades, and nearly everyone who has come into contact with the wounded person has had to pay for the pain of that person, until the person who owns the wound is willing to take responsibility for the wound and work it until it no longer controls her.

It's pretty easy to anesthetize ourselves in a myriad of ways, trying not to feel the agony in our souls. We drink and drug our pain away, causing ourselves even more pain, for the truth is that our addictions are anxiety-management techniques that ultimately not only don't work, but create for us even more pain.

We numb ourselves with food or being busy. We use shopping and television as drugs. We run from one event to another, from one relationship to another, seeking relief from that which has us all knotted up. Sometimes we hide our pain in religion or God-talk, hoping to escape the realities of our lives.

Sometimes we throw money at the problem, and if there is a lot of money to be thrown, facing the problem head-on can be avoided for a long time. Admittedly, money helps ease much of the discomfort of hard times, and it is a lot easier to suffer when you don't have to worry about how you will pay for it. Ultimately, however, there comes a time when we have to admit that there isn't enough money to make the pain go away.

Some people try to control or repair the problem, and when what they do doesn't work, they do more of it. Some study the problem and form careers trying to gain some authority over that which hurt them, becoming doctors or ministers, therapists or legal experts. Some people work harder and longer, running faster and faster for as long as they can until, finally, if they are fortunate, they bottom out and come to the place of admitting that they are powerless over the thing they have spent a lifetime trying to avoid or change.

We sing the blues, we whine and complain, we become victims and martyrs—or heroes!—trying to manage the pain that won't go away. We try to explain it and understand it; we make pronouncements about our own particular kind of pain, and sometimes we start movements or nonprofits or write books to try to get on top of the thing that keeps pushing us down into the depths of suffering.

If we are fortunate, however, there comes a time when all of our ways and means of avoiding ourselves and our agony fail, and we are brought to the mat of our own ash heap and must make a hard decision about that pain that will not go away. If we will, we can choose to *suffer* the thing we cannot change.

*

"Why do you keep on doing that over and over?"

It was a clear, perfect spring morning, and the sun danced on the walls of the sacred space where I had landed, hoping to find *the answer*. I was sick and tired of repeating the same mistake, but I couldn't seem to stop myself.

I sat for a long time, reflecting on the fact that, indeed, my current behavior was not solving my problem, no matter how many times I repeated it or how much I had perfected that thing that wasn't working. It didn't matter how good I was at explaining things or how fervently I worked on my self-devised treatment plan—the pain I was carrying would not go away, and I could not solve my own problems.

"I thought that it would finally . . . work," I stammered, and my questioner burst out laughing.

"Don't you know that that is the definition of insanity? Doing something over and over and expecting a different result is insanity."

I could feel myself blushing. I thought I was smarter than this! Indeed, I knew that I was going to have to change my ways, and I was scared to death. Little did I know that I was going to have to face my earliest emotional programming, my lifelong life script and all of the decisions I had made out of an early, deep wounding.

I had always known, at some level, that I was going to take the journey that lay ahead of me. Indeed, I had even yearned for that journey, for the truth is that God-who-works-within is always pushing us toward wholeness and confronting us with all of those things that prevent the work of redemption within us. I knew that I was going to have to face that *one thing* that had shaped my life, but, faced with the journey that lay ahead, I was both terrified and ecstatic.

I had recently been introduced to a new understanding of the word "suffering," and I knew that I was going to have to "suffer" this wound and that it was mine and only mine to suffer.

Examining the etymology of the word "suffer," you see that it comes from the Latin and carries the meaning of "bearing" something or "carrying it" and holding it from the bottom or from below. To suffer something, then, means that you "stand under it," holding it from below, until you understand it. The process of suffering, then, is a process of coming to understand; once you understand, there is great freedom.

Face-to-face with my life, I realized that I was being invited to "suffer" my own childhood wound, to face it in a new way, to hold it and carry it from the bottom or the cause of it. I was being called into the process of "standing under" my own life's burden by exploring and analyzing it, talking about it and examining it long enough to understand it.

I left that sacred space to go home, but I could make it only to St. Anne's Church. I parked beside the rose garden and made my way up to the large wooden door. Silently, I walked into that beautiful place where I loved to pray. This time, I barely made it to my favorite spot, where I pulled down the kneeling bench and fell to my knees, tears streaming down my face.

And there, in that quiet place, I abandoned my troubled heart and my stubborn will one more time to the Source, the Comforter/Confronter, the Guide, the Mystery, the Ornery God who had pursued me to this point, pushing me from within by my pain and beckoning to me from without by the Mystery.

God is truly ornery, I thought, there on that kneeling bench, because he will not let me go. God will not leave me alone until I fall onto this ash heap and suffer my life experience. It is radical love that makes God ornery, a love that is not satisfied until we face the truth and tell the truth and then, finally, have the courage to live the truth.

With my prayer of surrender, I didn't know where I was going or how I was going to survive the journey, but something—and *Someone*—within me began to stir, and I knew I had just enough faith to take the next step.

The next morning, just as I was waking, an image of a flame being re-ignited somewhere deep within the center of my soul was the first thought of the day, and I knew that I would be guided through the darkness. Even then, for a fleeing moment, I knew that I was being guided home to my authentic self.

If we will, we can choose to suffer the things we cannot change.

Most of us think of the word "suffering" as a noun, thereby concretizing our sorrows. Suffering is something we "have," something we have caused, or something that someone has done to us. In Christian circles, the idea that our sufferings are our punishment often swarms around people who are hurting. "If only you would pray harder or have more faith," we are told, adding shame for not being a good enough pray-er or a good enough person to the already unbearable problem. When we do use the word as a verb, we often use is as if suffering is an act of hopelessness.

To suffer something, in the context of *sitting strong*, however, means to choose to carry your pain consciously, to go into it intentionally and purposefully, to "stand under it" until you understand it. In other words, instead of becoming the victim of life's hurts so that you are hurt not only by the event but also by the way you "carry" what has happened to you, it is possible to move deeply into your pain, to feel that pain all the way to the fierce and ragged edges, to fully accept the hurt, and to integrate what has happened to you into your life story. Then, with the grace of God at work, you can be transformed by that which could have destroyed you.

It is possible, with time and the tedious work of becoming conscious, to carry that very thing that you thought you could not bear in such a way that you do find meaning in that which seems the most absurd. It is possible to "work your wound," to examine it, to approach it with a holy curiosity and reverence, to explore how it happened, to ask the hardest questions about it. It is possible to "suffer" your losses, to "suffer" your agony, to "suffer" your fate and your defects in such a way that, finally, you do find where God is at work.

Whining and singing the blues are not authentic suffering.
Complaining and blaming are not authentic suffering.
Regressing to a childish state, expecting others to take care of you and hiding out in some bunker of defensiveness are not authentic suffering.
Resisting and being stoic are not authentic suffering, and neither do they reveal courage or bravery.
Going bravely into your pain, trembling though you may be, is authentic suffering.
Sitting strong—*facing the truth, telling the truth, living the truth, and doing all of that with as much consciousness as you can is* authentic *suffering.*

Suffering something, carrying it until you find the meaning in it, allows you to expand your image of who God is. It allows you to expand your image of who you are and your image of the world and how you are to be in it. It requires you to grow up.

Suffering something consciously will refine you and make you more compassionate and wise. It sets us free from inordinate attachments. It helps us to detach from our idols and to separate the important from the trivial.

Authentic suffering rejects simplistic answers to complex issues. It recoils in the face of sentimental tripe, and it avoids premature and easy pronounce-ments about "why this happened." Suffering certainly shudders in holy hesitation before announcing what the Almighty has in mind.

Conscious suffering takes time, and it will not be rushed. It has its own process and its own timetable. Those who rush the process so that they or

19

somebody else will *feel better* will discover that the wisdom in the wound will reveal itself when it is ready.

The truth is that what is buried alive, stays alive, and so responsible and mature adults are called to deal with the pain in their lives in such a way that they will not inflict their pain onto others. Not dealing with those things that are huge in our lives, keeping them buried, exacts a price, and it is often our loved ones who pay the most severe price.

Coming to consciousness about what it is that hurts is an act of kindness and a moral obligation. Over the years, on the ash heap, I have learned an important lesson: *What you do not work out or talk out, you will project out or act out or take out on someone else.*

*

There is an old story about a Chinese farmer whose horse ran away. The villagers made a trek to his farm to offer him sympathy, and he said to them, "How do you know this is bad luck?"

The next day, the farmer's horse came back, and with that horse, four others!

The villagers returned to the farm to congratulate him, and he said, "How do you know this is good luck?"

The next day, the farmer's only son, trying to tame the new horses, fell and broke his leg, and sure enough, here came the villagers, to offer their condolences. Again, the farmer asked, "How do you know this is bad luck?"

The next month, war broke out in the land, and the farmer's son, because of his broken leg, was not able to go off to war!

We could, obviously, take the farmer's story on and on, but the point is made. We cannot know, in the middle of something, what is "bad" and what is "good." We do know what hurts, if we allow ourselves to feel our own pain, and we know that being human contains both joy and sorrow and that it is, indeed, a sometimes painful venture, fraught with danger and disease, loss and suffering.

When life hurts, we can "suffer" what hurts and be transformed by it, if we are willing to.

It is also the Chinese who have taught us that there is in every crisis an opportunity, and much of what and who we become is based on how we respond to what happens to us.

And much of what happens to us is shaped by whether or not we allow God to be with us in the suffering, and that willingness is based on how and who we believe God to be.

20

The God Problem

I would not believe in a God I could define.
—Pittman McGehee

In the beginning, God created man in his own image, and ever since,
man has been returning the favor.
—Mark Twain

It is a dreadful thing to fall into the hands of the Living God.
—Hebrews 10:31

One of the most riveting moments in the award-winning television series *The West Wing* takes place in the magnificence of Washington National Cathedral, at the funeral of President Josiah Bartlet's secretary, who had also been his father's secretary when he was young. The character, Mrs. Landingham, had been a kind of moral compass for Bartlet for much of his life, and the funeral scenes were interspersed with flashbacks of conversations between the two of them.

At the end of the funeral, Bartlet asks everyone to leave him alone and seal the cathedral. Walking slowly up the center aisle, the President confronts God with his raw agony and grief.

"She bought her first new car and you hit her with a drunk driver," he says. "What, was that supposed to be funny?"

"Have I displeased you, you feckless thug?" he asks, and then he names the good things he has done, demanding, "That's not enough to buy me out of the doghouse?"

For those of us who tremble and quake in the face of the holiness of God, this scene and its language disturbs our sensibilities. For those of us who were brought up in traditions that discouraged even *saying* the name of God, this character's boldness in the face of God forces us to face the intimacy question with God.

Am I on intimate enough terms with the Creator to stand up to him and tell him the truth about the way I feel?

Do I trust God enough to rail and rant and rave to him when life hurts so much I think I cannot bear it? Do I trust myself with God enough to speak what I am really feeling to him?

Is my faith in the Source strong, like the biblical characters who wrestled and tangled with God, or do I prefer a wimpy, bumper-sticker theology that keeps God small and manageable?

When life crashes in on me, what do I do with the terrible feeling that God has, somehow, let me down?

Which is more nearly prayer, outrageous honesty that minces no words or sweet piety that covers an angry, bitter heart?

There is, perhaps, nothing that happens between human beings that hurts as much as a betrayal by someone who was supposed to love you, protect you, or be faithful to you. When that betrayal happens, all of the fault lines of the relationship are exposed, and the truth about the relationship comes roaring to the surface. It is a terrible thing to be betrayed by someone we have loved and trusted with our secrets and our sorrows, our bodies and our beliefs, our hopes and our hurts, our love and our life. Who among us has not been disappointed by another human being? Indeed, each kind of betrayal between human beings has its own bitter taste and aftertaste.

Worse, indeed, is that terrible feeling when all you have ever believed about God comes crashing to the ground. There is perhaps nothing more disturbing and disorienting than to be faced with one of life's unspeakable horrors or grave losses and, with it, that terrible feeling of being betrayed by God.

Which one of us who has lived through one of life's horrific tragedies has not felt the confusion of being thrown to the mat as much by the crashing of our ideas about who we thought God was going to be as by the tragedy?

Where is "sweet Jesus, meek and mild" at the grave of a child?

What happened to the "Lover of my soul" when all that I had counted on has been stripped from me?

Sadly, many people, in the face of life's largest God problems, choose to become cynical or skeptical, often deciding that agnosticism or atheism are far safer paths than belief in God. Or many continue to go through the motions of religious life as practical atheists, but using other gods to soothe their ragged edges. Some suppress their deepest questionings because to struggle and wrestle with God is simply too hard. God is, after all, a daunting force with which humans contend.

Poor Job. You have to feel sorry for the guy. At the opening of his story, he looks so good, operating under the practices of regular worship, faithful sacrifices, obedient service to God-as-he-understood-him, confident that if he would do those righteous things, God would watch over him and protect him and continue to make him prosper.

How could it be that such a fine man could make such a quick trip from the peak of his performance to the ash heap of humiliation and loss? What did he do to fall out of favor with God so fast? And what does it say about God, after all, that he would let one of his good ones get into such a mess?

Did God turn his back on Job, and if God did do that, what kind of God would do such a thing?

Did God just dislike this man?

Was it God who was the problem? Or Job?

Or, perhaps, was it Job's *ideas* about God that were the problem? Was his God-concept so skewed, so immature, so flawed, so inadequate that his whole life was "off," for it seems to be true that whatever a human being believes and feels about God and who God is in relation to him is vitally important.

Indeed, Job's assignment on the ash heap placed him in a terrible struggle with God and with who he had believed God to be. All of his notions about God were turned upside down. Everything he had believed and practiced in his religious life was challenged by the God who wanted more for him.

The image of God that is revealed in the book of Job is different from the one in the earlier books of the Old Testament, and certainly, the person of Jesus is, for Christians, the best picture of God that we have. Yet the ancients seemed to accept the fact that struggling and wrestling with God was part of what it meant to be human, and that the struggle itself had, in a sense, a touch of the heroic in it. Maybe we humans cannot become fully human until we have a wrestling match with the Almighty.

Prior to the book of Job, the children of Israel related to God primarily as children relate to a father figure. They were led by religious leaders who had a more mature and direct relationship with Yahweh than they did.

In the book of Job, however, suddenly God moves directly into the life of an individual and, instead of blessing and protecting "his child," allows his servant to be tested and tested severely.

Sitting on that ash heap, Job most certainly was stunned by the way God had allowed him to be stripped of everything that had given him meaning and purpose. Surely, Job was in shock, for he had counted on God to notice the consistency of his ritual sacrifices and the faithfulness of his worship! Surely, God had thrown Job a curve, and it must have been humiliating, embarrassing, devastating, and confusing for Job to have to sit with his current state and wrestle with who God was to him.

*

Roaming through the antiquities in the British Museum last spring, I came upon a crude and worn statue that had once stood outside an ancient village. "There is no other god but this one," proclaimed the writing on the statue, according to the information printed beside it. Apparently, the statue and its pronouncement were intended to keep anyone else from bringing their "god" into the space presided over by this roughly hewn, crudely shaped "god."

What a pitiful, paltry god! I thought to myself, moving on through the displays. *How could that crudely carved statue provide any kind of protection?* I wondered. And yet, in many ways, that "god" is no different from some of the idols we "sophisticated," modern people look to for solace and salvation. We are so desperate for meaning and so devoid of heroes and heroines that we try to turn almost anything into a god, "worshiping" at various man-made altars and then insanely starting wars over whose god is the real god.

Indeed, God has always been one kind of problem or another to his creatures, so much so that people will try to pretend that there is no God or they will make gods of substances, other people, and processes, trying to find meaning in whatever they can achieve, acquire, or accomplish.

God was most certainly a problem for Job, and God is often a problem for me, but I have an idea that, at times, much of the problem is the result of my faulty and frail images of who God is.

God is a problem for us humans when we make God too small, when we misrepresent the nature of God, and when we get all mixed up and forget that God is the Creator and we are the creatures—not the other way around!

The truth is that there is no other concept that human beings hold that is more important than the God-concept, and the fact is that all of us have an operative concept of who God is, but most of us have not brought that concept to consciousness.

*

Leaving the British Museum, a long-forgotten memory from my freshman year of college came back to me. Slipping onto the elevator in my college dorm, just as it closed, and hoping I could get into my room before "room check," a notion that now sounds as anachronistic and outdated to me as some of my earlier concepts of God, I hit the button that would take me to the sixth floor of Ruth Collins Hall and then leaned against the wall of the elevator for the slow, shaky ride.

Directly in front of me was a poster announcing the theme of the upcoming Religions Emphasis Week at Baylor University. A serious-looking being, pointing his finger outward, obviously in my direction, asked, in bold font, "Who do YOU say that I am?"

At the time, the most interesting part of my freshman experience was my social life, but I have never forgotten that poster or the question. In fact, for most of my adult life, I have been riveted by that question of Jesus' to his closest friends and disciples. Indeed, how one answers that question shapes, in many ways, the way one lives her life.

Little did I know, when I was eighteen, that the questions about God and the problems with God would become a dominant theme and part of my lifework for all of my adult life.

Like Job, I have been brought to my knees since that encounter with Jesus' big question in the dorm elevator. Like Job, I have found that the childhood or adolescent image I had of God is not adequate for the challenges of my adult life. Indeed, even the concept of God that I had a year ago isn't big enough, for God is continually leading me out onto the razor's edge of risks I had not planned on taking and showing me still more of his nature, still more of his greatness and even more of a larger world than I had previously imagined.

As a person who speaks *about* God a lot, which is different from speaking *for* God, I naively used to believe that we were all talking about the same Being.

In my early adulthood, when I was first introduced to the Twelve Steps of Alcoholics Anonymous, I was stunned. I could accept the part about "turning my life and will over to the care of God," but I almost choked over that "as I understand him" part.

I was stunned because that was the first time it had ever occurred to me that everyone didn't understand God as I understood God. As much as I hate to admit it, I believed that my way was "the right way" to think about God.

In my childhood and adolescence, and even into my early adulthood, I understood that there were "people of other religions" who worshiped God in strange ways, but I assumed that the people with whom I worshiped and worked shared the same image of God.

Once I got to adulthood and experienced the conflicts even within my denomination over the nature of God and the interpretation of the Bible, I began to understand in a hurry that we were approaching the most sacred aspects of life from totally different perspectives.

Say the name "God," for example, in a group of people, and you will come up with as many different images of God as there are individuals, and the truth is that when we begin to talk about the Holy One, all we really can talk about is our own ideas, images, and concepts of God. Sometimes those images of God that we carry in our heads and hearts are life-giving and sometimes they are not. Sometimes the God-image is a helper, and sometimes a hindrance, and much depends on experiences a person has had about people who represented God or who taught her about God.

Part of the problem with a person's God-concept is that that concept is formed unconsciously and non-rationally, early in the child's life, and it is based on the earliest caregiver or authority figure. God is "like" our parents, our first deities, and if they were caring and trustworthy, it is easy to form an image of a God who can be trusted. If the parents or caregivers were absent, abusive, or inconsistent in their care, negligent or preoccupied, then the child is going to conclude that that is how God is.

Often, when working as a spiritual director, a directee will say to me, "I do not believe in God," and it is my job to invite the person to tell me about "the god you don't believe in." Nearly always, I will come to the point of saying, "I don't believe in that god either," and then the foundational work of discerning the direction of the Spirit in the person's life can begin as we form, together, a God-image that will work.

"You may have to fire that god!" I sometimes tell directees when they describe a punitive, punishing God.

"Wouldn't you rather have a God-concept that nourishes and supports you?" I sometimes ask when a person is working with an image of God as slave-driver. Apparently, Job's image of God required him to be good and to do good; in response, Job would have the protection and provision due a loyal and faithful subject.

*

When I was a child, I believed that God was a glorified man, likely sitting on a big throne (much like Abraham Lincoln in Washington, DC), fixed and sort of concretized in one place, watching over me. Because of my religious culture, I also believed that that big, powerful, fixed God had a huge "Lamb's Book of Life" in his lap, and every time I did something I shouldn't do, he would make a big black mark by my name, and of course, my sins would be read out for all to hear at judgment day!

Out of my own particular family and religious history, I have had to work hard to separate the man behind the pulpit, who happened to be my own earthly father, from God. Separating that earliest deity, the parent, from God is a task for all of us, but for preacher's children, there is a particular uniqueness to the process.

How different and childish that idea is to the idea of God as the animating force, emanating throughout creation, or the idea of God as ground of our being, the "one in whom it all hangs together"! And what about the idea, shocking as it is, that God is the force of unconditional love, drawing all people to wholeness, health, and abundance?

I know that my image of God is still too small, and I acknowledge that sometimes I want to make God in my image so that I can manage and control him. Sometimes I have to admit that I diminish God so that I can maintain my own presumed authority over my own life, and sometimes I keep God small and in a box of my own personal doctrine because I am afraid of the magnificence and sovereignty of God. Maybe I'm even afraid of the love of God.

In today's culture, two predominant God-concepts seem to be sweeping through this country. One image of God is that of the rule-maker and judge; the other is the benevolent Santa Claus. Both of these images lead to theologies based on lies and distortions, keeping people scared and self-righteous, on the one hand, and entitled and addicted to the buzz of sensationalism and the promise of special privileges. Each expression of the distortions of who God is reflects a half-truth; each keeps people childish and dependent upon a religious institution outside of themselves instead of encouraging them to encounter the challenge of the "kingdom of God within."

I would love to sit back and poke fun at the "prosperity gospel" preachers who have sold their promises and their programs on television for the past twenty years. I would love to be able to say that I am so sophisticated that I don't bargain with God, hoping that God will bless me for all of my service to him, but the hard truth is that underneath all of my adult trappings resides a little girl who still wants a father figure to watch over me. Inside all of my lofty ideas about God, there is still a child, desperately wanting the protection and provision of a God who thinks I am his "special pet" or his "favorite daughter."

I would love to adopt the God of fundamentalism that says that if only I would adhere to "these right beliefs," I would be safe from harm, and I long to be able to take the cross out of Christianity, losing myself in the feel-good, cotton-candy entertainment that masquerades as religion and "church," but the Scriptures pull me back over and over to this troublesome God who will not let go of us until we have let go of all the gods that aren't God.

I would love to make God over in my image, and God knows I've tried! However, God, who loves unconditionally and who is attempting to heal and transform, liberate and empower me by his unrelenting, ruthless love, will not leave me like I am with my lesser gods.

I cringe and withdraw from the God of rules and legalism. I almost break out in hives when doctrine and dogma are used to intimidate and infantilize human beings. I run from any kind of system that portrays a vengeful, punishing God who cracks the whip of fate wherever it pleases him to do so. I reject the concept of a Deity who capriciously causes hurricanes and tsunamis and brings down terrorist attacks and cancer on the innocents of the world.

*

A person's image of God is the most important image she has, for it shapes the way she relates to herself and to other people, and to the world. From the image of God that a person holds is formed the self-image.

A serious path that leads to wholeness and health requires time and effort to reflect on who God is. When people do not take time to examine the nature of God for themselves, they are likely to live and make choices with a God-concept that they have brought with them from childhood. Today's challenges cannot be met adequately by yesterday's answers, and a three-year-old understanding of God simply isn't adequate for the challenges of an adult world. Without self-reflection and intentional study, persons will accept any idea of God that the loudest, most seductive or persuasive voice happens to be selling at the moment.

The truth is that suffering introduces you to your God-concept in a hurry. If you are willing to reflect on what that concept is, you will, in a crisis, generally find that your God is too small. Furthermore, in a crisis, it is a common human tendency to regress to an earlier stage of development.

One of the methods God uses to expand our image of him is to challenge our current concept of who he is. And that isn't an easy process.

I cannot find any of the great souls who did not wrestle mightily with God, and part of the reason for the wrestling, starting with Jacob and his wounding angel, it seems to me, is that all they had believed God to be and what God wanted of them continually put them in conflict with their own ego positions or the common human need to conform to one's culture

*

Out there on the ash heap, Job's first assignment was to face his idea of who he was to God. He had counted himself as one of God's friends, yet it was clear that God had allowed the most severe losses possible to come into his life.

What was Job to do but despair? How could Job have done anything but surrender to the agony of the betrayal and his losses? What more could he do than to fall, helpless and broken, onto the ash heap and wait to die?

The story is told of Teresa of Avila, Spanish mystic, author of great spiritual classics, and reformer of the church of the thirteenth century. One day, as she was out and about in her buggy, reforming the church and helping people know God, her horse tripped, turning her buggy over and throwing Teresa out into the mud.

Picking herself up out of the mud, the great saint of the church shook her fist toward the heavens and said, "If this is how you treat your friends, no wonder you have so few of them!"

And, of course, more recently, it was Mother Teresa who said, in response to someone's pious quoting of the Scripture about how God will not give us more than we can handle, "I wish the Lord didn't trust me quite so much."

Surely, Job must have felt the same way, out there on the ash heap, contemplating his interrupted and shattered life and the shattering of his ideas of who God was to him and who he was to God.

God is not, we finally discover, the ultimate bulletproof vest. Indeed, for every one of us, no matter how faithful we are to our rituals and rites and regardless of how much tithe we give or how many good deeds we perform, even God bows to our free will and to the laws of nature that he ordained. As much as I hate to face it, all of my goodness does not build a hedge high enough to protect me or my children from the plight and peril of being human.

My friend and mentor, the author Madeleine L'Engle, quoted the following ditty when addressing the issues of suffering at a writer's retreat at Laity Lodge, on the Frio River of Texas: "The rain, it falleth everywhere, on the just and the unjust fellow . . . but more, it seems, on the just, for the unjust have the just's umbrella!"

*

Following my three-year training program at the Spiritual Direction Institute at the Cenacle Retreat Center in Houston, Texas, I asked Sister Mary Dennison to guide me through the Nineteenth Annotation of the Spiritual Exercise of St. Ignatius. Each week, I made my way through the city to the quiet retreat center in one of the busiest sections of the city, and each week, Sister Mary guided me to go deeper and deeper into my life with God.

It was that year, oddly enough, that I faced the greatest personal crises of my life. I thought, frankly, that that was profoundly unfair of God, yet Sister Mary gently guided me back, over and over, to the same two questions. Sister Mary's questions forced me to rethink and reform my image of God, hopefully bringing my consciousness of God to a more mature and adult level. "Who are you to God? " Sister Mary would ask me, over and over, "and who is God to you?"

The exquisite gift of tragedy and trauma is right in the terrible pain of it. Trouble really does force you to face the places where you have entrapped God in doctrine or ritual, encasing the Almighty in the trappings of the past or the limitations of your own imagination.

Over and over, on my own ash heap of suffering, I pushed at those questions, or maybe it was that the life-giving spirit of God at work in me in places I couldn't even recognize, dismantling my old system of beliefs and gently guiding me out into a larger world of mystery and the mysterious. I was being led, and sometimes forced, to an encounter with the Holy One, who sometimes chooses to turn our comfortable and cozy worlds upside down so that we can grow up and grow into the largeness of our own lives.

I have come to understand that, in a way, God evolves as human consciousness evolves, and that the understanding of God held by the people in Genesis was an infantile image of God. Job, in the very middle of the biblical revelation, represents a shift in the God-concept, a maturing of the relationship between individuals and the Almighty, and an example of the reality that God is always ushering us out beyond what we thought we could be or do, and sometimes the method God works best in is trial and trouble.

I don't believe that God caused Job's suffering any more than I believe that God caused mine.

I don't believe that God wills for one person's son to be killed in an accident, but spares someone else's, and I cringe in the face of the platitudes well-meaning people offer in the presence of tragedy.

The reality is that all of the answers to why people suffer and why bad things happen to good people are cold comfort when you are in the middle of suffering.

However, I continue to learn and relearn, as I walk through suffering with others, and as I have suffered my own losses, that God is in the middle of our sufferings, attempting to bring about good, in spite of everything we do to get in his way.

*

Following the tragedy of terrorism inflicted on New York City, I happened to be teaching the book of Job on Wednesday nights at South Main Baptist Church in Houston. At the end of each session, a particular man repeatedly challenged my assumptions about the goodness of God, and I had to admit that the evidence he presented was compelling.

"If God is good," he continued to ask, "why does he let these horrible things happen? If God is love, why doesn't he stop the suffering?"

"Sometimes it's not about why God lets these things happen," I said one night, exhausted from the intellectual arguments. "Sometimes we have to take a look at why we humans participate in behaviors that allow the suffering of others!"

"The goodness of God is present in all things," I argued, "and it is up to us to look for it and cooperate with it."

No matter what I tried to sell, the man didn't buy it, and I finally had to admit that, with him at least, I wasn't getting anywhere.

One night, a woman came up to me after the lively exchange between the doubter and me. She was a cancer patient from another city, getting treatment at M. D. Anderson Cancer Center and staying in one of the apartments the church provides for people from other cities who have to receive treatment over a long period of time.

Over the course of the study of Job, she had sat at the very edge of the crowd. Now, she wore the telltale turban. She had become pale and weak, and yet there was a light in her eyes and a brilliance to her smile that dazzled me.

"Don't stop affirming the goodness of God," she said to me, and then she simply knocked me over with her simple affirmation of faith.

"You know, I'm not going to live," she continued, "and I'm at the bottom, but what I have discovered is that it is people who have been to the bottom who learn that God is there, right there with us, and that God is love."

*

Some people, when trouble hits, draw nearer to God, and some people run away. Some, in the face of tragedy, become bitter, while others allow the Living God to burn away all that is dross so that the brilliance of the gold that is within them shines even more brightly. Some people make it through the time on the ash heap, and some don't.

It is one thing to trust God when things are going your way, your guy is President, and all your children are doing what they are supposed to be doing, at the moment. It's another thing to trust God when everything you valued has been taken from you.

Job sat on that ash heap and wrestled hard with God, not knowing what the outcome of his wrestling would be, and that is radical trust. In his weakness, Job *sat strong*, but while he was sitting, he worked hard.

*

The German poet Rainer Maria Rilke wrote the following words to a young poet in response to a letter:

> I beg you . . . to have patience with everything unresolved in your heart and try to love the questions themselves as if they were locked rooms or books written in a very foreign language. Don't search for the answers, which could not be given you now, because you would not be able to live them. And the point is, to live everything. Live the questions now. Perhaps then, someday far in the future, you will gradually, and without even noticing it, live your way into the answer.

I discovered that in the middle of difficulty, there is always a question, which, when addressed, enlarges and enriches my entire life, and so I have come to live into those questions and see where they take me.

What is being asked of you about your image of God?
What is being asked of you about your own life?
What do you need to face that you have avoided?
To what are you attached that you need to release?

If God is at work in your innermost being and in your circumstances, attempting to enlarge your heart, how are you holding God hostage to a childish or immature concept of God?

What limited and limiting belief about yourself and about your own life is keeping you stuck?

Going into the darkness, asking the hard questions, sitting strong are not guarantees of meeting God and finding meaning in the suffering, but not working the wound is a sure bet that you won't find the meaning.

Oh, God—
        excuse me,
but I really hadn't planned on
getting to know you quite so well.
                I'd really planned on waiting
                a few more years before
I spent so much time with you—
                I wanted to run the show myself
                for a little while longer . . . and
I had some things to do, you know—
                some places I wanted to go, people
                to meet, worlds to explore, fun
                to have—before
I got serious about
knowing you.
                Don't you get it, God? I wanted to be on my own for a
while!

A simple Sunday morning acquaintance
                really was enough for me, God,
        but you have gone and messed that up . . .
or maybe I did, or life did, or,   **oh, whatever!**

Whatever has happened, you've got my attention now.
This problem won't go away. *It will not go away.*
I can't find an answer, and I can't even find
anyone who has an answer . . .
and you keep nagging me awake
in the middle of the night,
and I have to sit here in this
awful darkness while you
torment me with this thing I cannot bear . . .
and the answers I do not have . . .
and the silence that screams at me,
      keeping me from sleeping.
            All I really wanted of you, God,
            was just enough religion to have a good
life,
            but you seem to have another idea.

The Satan Problem

Evil is "live" spelled backward. Evil is in opposition to the life force. . .
It is that which kills spirit.
—M. Scott Peck

People who are always looking for the devil always find him!
—L. D. Ball

"I don't want to know this about God," a young woman told me after reading the first chapter of Job. She never came back to the Bible study that year.

"I can't accept that God would allow Satan this much power," said another. "This makes me unable to accept the Bible!"

"How am I supposed to trust God when he allowed Satan to do these awful things to a good man? What hope do I have?" demanded a seeker who had just stuck his toe in the sometimes roiling waters of Bible study.

Admittedly, it's easy to stumble on the conversations between Job and the devil, right there in the first couple chapters of the book of Job, and it is often there, unfortunately, that people stop reading and stop questioning. Sometimes it's just too hard to let your mind open itself to the possibility that God converses with Satan and, knowingly, allows Satan to mess with us!

The truth is that serious study of the Bible will push you out onto the razor's edge of intellectual risk, and the truth is that many don't want to face hard and complex issues any more than they want to face private and personal pain! In reality, most of us want our religion to make us feel better or more powerful in the face of the hardships and challenges of everyday life!

How is it, we ask, that a good God allows Satan into his counsel of angels?

And, if God is sovereign, omnipotent, and omniscient, why does he have to ask Satan where he has been? Doesn't God know?

Why does our loving God even entertain the idea of allowing Satan to "test" Job, who is, after all, a good man? Why doesn't God send Satan after one of the bad guys?

And how on earth do we common folks reconcile the dark side of God's nature with the light? How do we draw near to God, who may turn on us and allow us to be put in harm's way?

What about the question of how a good God could allow his own son to die a criminal's death? How can a good and merciful God allow innocent children to suffer? And how is it that bad things keep on happening to good people?

Indeed, it is much easier to slap a sentimental bromide over our pain, and others', in an attempt to avoid feeling the horror of it. It is so much easier to spout simplistic answers to complex problems than it is to face things as they really are, to tell the absolute, hard, unvarnished truth about things that we'd rather lie about.

Confrontation with pain and suffering does invite us into the process of facing what it is we believe about God, what we believe about the forces of evil, and what we believe about ourselves. Just as the book of Job has a way of explaining what happened to Job, we find our ways to explain our suffering to ourselves and others in order to survive.

*

Reading the book of Job through the eyes of history and in the days of modern science, and with a knowledge of how family systems work, we have to admit that we read Job's story as people who have come to expect good health and extreme safety. We expect our babies to be born healthy, and we demand that they have what they need to thrive and grow.

Parents today work hard to make sure that their children will not have any hardship We take our children to church and give them character education, hoping, just as Job did, to build a hedge big enough around them so they won't do what we don't want them to do. We want them to make us proud by earning awards and medals. In the American culture today, we assume that we and our children will live long and healthy lives.

When bad things happen to us, we quickly begin scurrying around to explain why they happened, often relying on childhood teachings that are not adequate for the hard stuff of adulthood. When we are hurting, we want answers. We want "the reason" for why it happened, and most of all, we want relief from the pain. If we can find something, *anything*, that makes us feel better, we will grab it and grasp it to our minds and hearts, trying to go back in time to that place of innocence when we believed that we were exempt from the pain of life.

Over and over, we are brought to confront the questions of how a good God can let innocent people suffer. We demand answers to why evil seems to be rewarded and why it is that God allows pain and suffering to continue. We shake our hands and cluck our tongues over God's seeming oblivion to our plight, when, in truth, we might do well to take a hard, long look at the times we have not done what we could have done and when we have done what we should not have done. Ultimately, we must look at the ways we have ignored the ways of God.

Finally, responsible people must ask, "How can a good God tolerate the willfulness, indifference, and outright defiance of human beings? How can God keep on blessing us when we ignore what we know is right over and over? How can God keep on being so patient with us, given our propensity to do what we know is wrong?"

The Hebrew people of the ancient world lived in closer proximity to the dangers and perils of nature, and they had their way of explaining the harshness of nature. They were more comfortable with the notion that God would be in conversation with Satan than we are. When bad things happened, they understood that "the Lord gives, and the Lord takes away."

Pushed to the ash heap, Job exemplifies a new level of consciousness, in that he didn't just accept the events, blindly rolling over, cursing God, and dying, as his wife suggested that he might do. Job could have just sat and scraped his sores with the shards of pottery lying around in the rest of the garbage until he died. He could have called for some kind of palliative to put him out of his misery. Instead, Job chose to sit with his agony, to go into it and feel it and to grapple with the hardest questions a human being has to face.

*

I have accepted that bad things happen to good people, but I do wrestle with the fact that God, who is omnipotent, does not stop some of the evil and harm that inflicts the innocent and injures the strong and the weak alike.

I am very careful about what I attribute to the devil. I take evil much too seriously to speak flippantly about the devil's work.

I am much too acquainted with my own delusions and illusions to make careless pronouncements about what the devil is doing.

And the reality of human freedom and our capacity to choose the downward pull staggers my imagination. That God continues to be patient with us is what amazes and confounds me.

*

"What do you wonder about?" the television interviewer asked the popular young media personality, a prominent preacher in a large church.

"Wonder?" the congenial fellow asked, looking off-camera. "I don't wonder about anything."

How nice! I thought. *Why can't I be like that?*

*

The truth is that trauma and trouble introduce us to ourselves by disorienting us and by throwing us off-course into that which is unfamiliar, uncharted, unpredictable, and, yes, unwanted, and it is natural, in the panic of the experience, to be confused and perplexed about everything.

When we are confused, we scurry to find stable ground, and we are often so desperate for that which is familiar that we will accept assurance from anyone who speaks with some voice of authority. We will latch on to answers from those who promise that they will take care of us, and we resort to temporary fixes just to get through the day. And yet our questions keep on bothering us, waking us up in the middle of the night, disturbing our peace, and demanding that we enter into the rigorous, painful process of facing our old, worn-out concepts of God.

> *Why did this happen?*
> *Why did it happen to me?*
> *Why did it happen now?*

In every crisis or trauma, whether it is a crisis of faith, a chronic illness, a devastating loss, or a coming to terms with one's own brokenness, we are provided the opportunity to ask those hard questions, and if we are to wring the blessing out of the pain, we must go into the pain and ask every single question that is lurking around in the shadows of our agony.

Asking these questions instead of blaming the devil leads to personal responsibility and can, ultimately, lead to freedom.

What am I going to do now?
How am I going to survive this?
Where is God now?
Why didn't God protect me?
If God is so powerful, why did he let this happen?
How can I possibly trust God if evil gets away with this?

In every problem and in every grief process, in our depressions and in our deepest moments of despair when we don't think we can continue, we are given the opportunity to face ourselves head-on and we are invited to allow God to break out of the small boxes into which we have confined him.

If you pick up the book of Job and can read through the two conversations between God and Satan and not be horrified and appalled, more power to you.

If you can explore the horrors of history and not wonder about the force of evil, then more power to you.

If, on the other hand, the problem of evil and the nature of God sometimes keep you awake at night, especially when it is your loved one who is hurting or your life that has been blown apart, Job is a good teacher in the tedious process of transformation.

It would be so easy and so comfortable to simply trust in the goodness of God and take life as it comes, but I am one of those who wrestles and twists and turns with life's happenings, trying to make sense of them. I wish I could just "let the river flow," quickly bless people who offend me, and bliss out in my religious trappings, but my fate has forced me to face hard questions and confront difficult issues about good and evil and God and Satan.

For the mind that does not accept ambiguity, ambivalence, and paradox, life is pretty simple, but the longer I live, the more I know that life is complex and complicated, messy and unpredictable, and any religious system or person who offers you relief from that reality is offering you unreality.

And any religious system or leader who seduces you into thinking that transformation can happen without sacrifice, surrender, or suffering is selling a lie.

*

So what does one do with this "conversation" between God and Satan? Do you interpret it literally, picturing a boardroom deliberation between Almighty God and a creature in a red suit with a pitchfork, horns, and a tail?

Or is it possible that taking the conversation and the story literally trivializes both the Bible and God? Is it possible that ancient people, attempting to explain why bad things happen to good people, chose to tell the story of Job, using a "conversation" between God and Satan? Perhaps the ancients were more comfortable with "the dark side of God" than we who want to lean on the unconditional love and free grace of Jesus are.

*

Whenever I teach the book of Job, I always ask, "How many of you have read the entire book of Job?" I always get the same paltry response. People may refer to "the patience of Job" or they may have some hint of an idea about what the book is about, but the truth is that very few people really know the book of Job, and part of the problem is in the very first chapter.

Eager Bible students gather to delve more deeply into the classic book on suffering, the book of Job, only to stumble in the very first chapter, give up, and put aside one of the world's great pieces of literature.

When I do discover persons who have dared to brave it all the way through what some call "the most sublime book of the Scriptures," I find that those persons have found within the book of Job depths of richness and meaning that are life-changing.

What is it about this book and this story that makes it one of the most quoted, and sometimes the most misquoted, books of the Bible? And why is it that many people stop short, right there in the first chapter, and never go back to grapple with the hard questions of evil and suffering and God's place in all of that?

Is it not the issues about good and evil, pain and suffering that stop people in their tracks? And aren't those the very issues, in real life, that stop us short?

*

Job was a good man and a "righteous" man, doing all the things that would keep up his good name with God, but there are lots of people who are "good."

His piety was such that he could assume prosperity and privilege in return, and yet all of the worst things that could happen to a man happened to Job. It was neither Job's piety nor his patience that makes this book and his story the source of endless fascination.

Scott Peck, in his landmark classic treatise on evil, *People of the Lie*, describes the conversation between himself and a client who has "made a deal with the devil": "You have a defect—a weakness—in your character, George," Peck told his patient. "Basically . . . you are a coward. Whenever the going gets a little bit rough, you sell out."

In Greek mythology, human hubris was the one thing the gods would not tolerate, yet in our culture we have become so confused by what is good and what is evil that we often wind up rewarding the very traits and practices that will, ultimately, come back to bite us in one way or another. Sadly, contemporary religion often colludes with evil instead of confronting it.

The growing common cultural deficiency in discerning the difference between good and evil is exacerbated by our need for instant gratification, our addiction to the quick fix and our love for sensationalism and power, all temptations that Jesus met and rejected in his torturous forty days in the wilderness.

Clearly, those who use others to advance their own agenda or plump up their pocketbooks, lying and manipulating figures and pretending one thing when the very opposite is true, are in the grips of a force that we must call evil.

*

On a hot summer afternoon, I bought a ticket at the River Oaks Theatre on West Gray, right on the edge of the neighborhood where top executives involved in the Enron collapse live. My husband and I settled down with our popcorn and soft drinks to watch the documentary movie on the Enron story, *Enron: The Smartest Guys in the Room*.

Friends had reported that when they had attended the movie, the theatre was full and the viewers, many of whom were likely to have been employees of Enron or friends of some of the main characters in the drama, watched in rapt silence. On opening night, I heard, the line for tickets wrapped around the block, and, just as it was the afternoon we saw the movie, people applauded the movie at the end of it.

However you interpret the events of the Enron collapse, it is pretty hard to avoid the appalling, overt, disgusting, and callous hubris of people who lied and manipulated, cavorted and partied, deceiving stockholders and employees and destroying the financial future of other human beings, all the time protecting themselves and, worse, maintaining their innocence and their "sympathy" for those who had lost their jobs and their retirement funds. Is there a clearer display of Scott Peck's theories of evil than the Enron story and its pack of lies?

Before I get too self-righteous and fall into my own hubris about "them," however, I have to face the fact of my own duplicities and lies. It isn't hard to identify the forces of darkness when the acts are so overt, violent, and obvious. It is hard, however, to differentiate between the more subtle forms of evil that often masquerade behind the glitter and sometimes even behind the "good." It is hard to identify evil within one's own life, to face the places where you are complicit with evil, either silently or directly.

I am compelled to look at the places in my own life where my walk and my talk don't line up and where I prefer a convenient and comfortable lie to the hard, cold, unvarnished truth, and there is nothing like pain and suffering to expose the fault lines of my own integrity.

If I am going to live in integrity, I must face the ways I deceive myself and others, pretending one thing and living something else. Ultimately, I will be brought face-to-face with those parts of my life where I have not been able to see or accept the truth about my own shadow and the ways in which I, either by the things I have done or the things I have left undone, colluded with the powers of evil.

The truth is that there is a Judas and a Hitler in every one of us. There is a murderer, a thief, a liar, and a prostitute in every human being that—in the right, or perhaps the wrong circumstances—can become a Hitler or worse. What is possible in any one of us is possible in all of us.

Perhaps the power of the book of Job is that we see in Job a person with the courage and stamina, the endurance and the perseverance to stand up to his troubles, to face head-on the agony of his losses, to endure the unbearable ravings of his "friends," and to wrestle with God. If evil triumphs when good people refuse to stand up to the hard stuff of life, Job is a vibrant, living, dynamic example of someone who can, indeed, take the hard stuff with the blessings.

It was Carl Jung who said, "The spirit of evil is negation of the life force by fear. Only boldness can deliver us from fear. If the risk is not taken, the meaning of life is violated." Indeed, there is radical boldness in Job's daring to endure the confrontation of his image of God with the disasters that struck him.

For the casual reader or for someone wanting light reading or a sweet devotional, Job is not the place to go. I have to admit that it's a little troubling to come upon that conversation between God and Job. It's disturbing to think about God agreeing to the devastating plans of the devil and, when God could, not preventing Job's troubles. The whole book throws all of the nice "teacup" images of God to the wind and rubs your nose in your sentimental ideas and images of who God is to you, and who you are to God.

Perhaps *holy boldness* is required just to face this "conversation" between God and Satan.

*

Serious scholars have explored the relationship between good and evil. Great thinkers get together in symposiums to try to find the answers and solutions to human suffering, and every great tragic event pushes some people to ask the painful questions that lead to some sense of peace with the issue of evil.

It is much easier to slap a pleasing platitude over our pain and others', in an attempt to avoid feeling the horror of it. It is so much easier to spout simplistic answers to complex problems and to hide in empty optimism that is based in denial than it is to face things as they really are. It is easier to lie than it is to tell the absolute, hard truth about the hard things of life, but *it is fear that keeps us bound in our lies and truth that will set us free.*

"I think I liked it better when I was in denial," I said to someone, and then I quickly said, "and yet staying asleep to the hard stuff makes me miss the wonders and the pleasures, the joys and the precious moments of grace."

One of the tasks on the ash heap is to ask the hard questions about the nature of evil and the problem of suffering, and the questions come to us like swords and machetes, cutting through our defenses and shattering our egos. It is appropriate to question God and to pour out your feelings and frustrations to God when you are thrown to the mat, unable to move.

The reality is that a confrontation with pain and suffering invites us into the hard process of facing what it is we believe about the forces of evil and what God has to do with evil. Our failures and our losses can provide an entry point of understanding of what we believe about ourselves and our place in the scheme of life.

On the ash heap of our own lives, we may discover the ways we have lied to ourselves about our own lives not because we are bad, but in order to survive.

*

God, you could have stopped this! Are you on sabbatical? My words were carried out of my mouth with the force of my sobbing. I thought I could not bear the pain I was carrying another minute, and I knew that the battle of my life really was a confrontation between good and evil; for the moment, it seemed that evil was going to win. The battle is not always so clear to me, but on this occasion, it felt as if God had abandoned me and my family to the forces of evil, and I was scared.

I have to admit it. I have trouble with the conversation between God and Satan because I want so desperately to be exempt from the influence of evil in my own life. I don't want to believe that God really would have a conversation with Satan. Not *my* God.

Evil exists, no matter how much we try to deny it, and the capacity for colluding with evil exists in all of us, not because we are "born bad," but because we have been given the awesome, sometimes terrible gift of free will.

We cannot have it both ways, so that we are free to choose and then, when we want it, coddled and cuddled by a benevolent God who won't let anything happen to his special favorites. We must learn, however, to discriminate between what is really evil and what is not.

When pushed to the ash heap, there is the opportunity to come to terms at a deeper level with the forces of evil and to differentiate between what is evil and what is just *life*.

The forces of nature—tsunamis, hurricanes, tornadoes, or floods—are not evil. They are simply nature. However, people who prey on the victims of natural disasters, taking advantage of their losses when they are vulnerable and using the disasters to feed their own greed and avarice, are participating with evil.

The death of an older person who has lived a long life is not a tragedy, but the fulfillment of a life. The death of a young person, in the prime of life, is a tragedy. The death of any person by an act of violence is participation with evil.

Expressing anger appropriately is not evil, and it can be a step in the process of reconciliation. The murder of another person's life force or the destruction of another person's dream through rage and violence, manipulation and control is participation with evil.

*

To work with other people to accomplish a task or a mission, to provide employment and opportunity for workers, to lead other human beings in a movement can be helpful and hopeful enterprises, contributing to the good of the whole. To use other people as objects, to manipulate other people to serve your needs, while neglecting theirs, and to oppress others in the service of an ideology is evil.

I know the power of evil to separate family members from each other.

I know the power of evil that works through duplicity and deceit.

I know how the unity of a church or a denomination can be destroyed by the perpetuation of a lie, told long enough, fervently enough, and by the "right people," in the right places, and at the right time.

I know what the evil of drugs can do to a bright young person with his whole future ahead of him.

I know what one seductive person, swabbing and polishing the ego of another, can do to destroy a marriage.

I am acutely aware of the subtle forms of manipulation and control that hide behind religious trappings. I know how the will of a person can be taken over by the misused power of an authority figure or a system that needs people to conform to its demands, no matter what.

I take evil seriously.

While I find naiveté charming on a child, I find it dangerous for an adult, for the inability to discern the difference between good and evil and a narcissistic need to hide out behind innocence and gullibility make adults vulnerable to being complicit with evil.

It is crucial that responsible people at least make an effort to discern the difference between that which is evil and that which is good.

The picture of the devil as a rubbery little creature in a red suit with horns, a tail, and a pitchfork trivializes the force of evil that operates in and among human beings. To interpret Satan literally as a force that is in other people or other systems and not accept the fact that every one of us is a potential carrier of evil is to be irresponsible.

Having grown up in the heart of conservative religion in the Bible belt, I heard enough hellfire and brimstone, "sinners in the hands of an angry God" sermons in my lifetime to numb my senses to the diatribes about the devil. People who are always yelling and screaming about other people's failings and sins are often exposed as carriers of the very thing they have been denouncing. Indeed, the power of projection is huge; the seduction to see in others what we cannot face in ourselves is natural for those of us who are human beings.

Jesus had it right when he said that we are prone to try to pick out the splinter in another's eye while we have a log in our own eye!

Who knows what kind of soul-searching went on in the mind and heart of Job, out there on that ash heap? Was there, in some way, a pride in him that made him trust in his own righteousness that he needed to face? Had he tried to cover up his children's lack of responsibility, infantilizing them by doing for them what they needed to do for themselves? Was there some way that he had trusted in his own goodness more than he trusted in the goodness of God?

Of course, the friends who were to come and question him provide us with a clue of what might have rumbled around in his mind, but one thing seems clear: by waiting it out on the ash heap, Job must have confronted his hardest questions.

*

A young mother, accused of abandoning her children in a car, was on trial for their death. In the prosecutor's opening statements, prior to the selection of the jury, he said, "You will have to decide if this horrible thing was done out of ignorance or negligence. You will have to decide if she knew what to do and simply chose not to do it, or if she thought that she could get by without being found out. Or did she, like so many of us, think that the laws that apply to everyone else did not apply to her?"

With my own issues of abandonment, I was relieved that I was not chosen for that jury panel, but I have devoted all of my adult life to a serious quest for the truth about what it is that makes me do what I do.

I do take seriously the evil that is "out there," but it is the capacity for evil that is within me that I must face, and every trip I make to the ash heap of despair or heartache, depression or loss, I must ask myself, "How did I get here? What did I do to participate in or perpetuate this problem? How am I responsible for what has happened? In what ways have the demons of anger and hate, shame and guilt, inferiority or fear, which make my inner kingdom their playground, operate in this situation? Am I, by my religious rituals and rites, attempting to bargain with God, hoping to avoid pain and punishment and gain the protection and blessings of God that I hope he will give to a good person like me? By my silences or by turning my head and not seeing what is in front of me, how do I collude with evil? How am I complicit with the use or abuse of other people as objects? What do I do to destroy another's sense of well-being?"

How willing am I to face the fact that anything that is in any human being is also in me? How willing am I to face the Hitler, the Judas, the murderer, or the thief in me that might be empowered to act to destroy others? How does a part of my own psyche turn, destructively and manipulatively, on the part of myself that is trying to do good?

*

On Tuesday nights, I attend classes taught by Dr. James Hollis, the executive director of the C. G. Jung Education Center. Through his teaching, I have come to understand the teachings of Jesus about the kingdom of God that is within us in a way I had never understood it before.

Repeatedly, through the years, I have heard Jim speak for the "moral obligation" each of us has to face our own shadow, to enter into our own darkness, and to take full responsibility for the ways in which we, inadvertently or deliberately, might be cooperating with evil or contributing to the pain of others.

The practice of "self-examination" is an ancient one. Taking a "Fourth Step," a fearless and searching moral inventory, is one of the ways out of addiction and into recovery. If I were running the world, I would insist that part of the curriculum for children of all ages would be classes on owning your own stuff, making amends, giving and receiving forgiveness and reconciliation, and I would reinstate the confessional booth as a regular discipline for human beings.

Knowing your own shadow and how it works, being conscious enough to be able to tell the difference between what is your stuff and that of another, acknowledging your own character defect and what makes you vulnerable to being taken over by your dark side are essential traits of mature and healthy, responsible human beings.

In fact, self-awareness is not self-absorption; instead, self-awareness prevents self-absorption. Self-understanding is not narcissism; instead, it is, as Jim Hollis reminds us repeatedly, one of the kindest things we can do for other people.

I have to believe that on the ash heap, Job took a long, hard, piercing, unrelenting look at himself.

Job is a model for us because he had the courage to face himself. He faced the evil in himself, and he refused to take the easy road out of his suffering, and in facing the darkness, Job opened the possibility of being transformed, healed, liberated, and empowered.

But transformation didn't happen overnight.

Oh, God—
    teach me to discern the
difference between good
and evil.   It seems that is should be so
        obvious, and yet
sometimes evil masquerades
as good, and sometimes good

47

looks like evil, and often
it's not so clearly defined
as I would like for it to be.

Teach me
not so much to look around me and outside
myself, but
within my own
dark chambers.
Show me the places where
I am
vulnerable to
the evil one, who
denigrates and destroys life.

Make it clear to me
when I am projecting
my own fears onto
someone out there . . .
making another
my scapegoat.

Make it clear to me
when I am full of anger and hate
so that I don't place
on another one of your precious creatures
the darkness that seethes
inside my own heart.

Beam your light into my darkness, Light of Lights.
Reveal that which I hide from myself.
Give me the courage to see what I cannot bear to see.
Remove from me the evil
that I allow to wound
any part of your creation,
including my own precious life.
Oh, God, may I never forget you and your truth,
for it is only in you that my safety lies.

Chapter Four

The Long Sit

There are situations in which the only correct adaptation
is patient endurance.
—CARL JUNG

Be great at the wait. Be patient. The ability to persevere is what
separates the whiners from the winners.
—OPRAH WINFREY

They that wait upon the Lord will renew their strength.
They shall mount up with wings like eagles. They shall run and
not be weary. They shall walk and not faint.
—ISAIAH 40:31

We dare not get rid of the pain before we have learned
what it has to teach us.
—RICHARD ROHR

When Lindy and Larry Neuhaus's son, Bo, died of cancer, they were instrumental in helping establish a center which was named for him, Bo's Place, to provide a place where children can come and, with caring adults and other children, work through the terrible effects of the death of a parent, sibling, or friend. Each year, I look forward to attending the luncheon that benefits Bo's Place, and this year former Secretary of State James Baker III delivered a powerful speech about the impact of his wife's death on his life and that of their four sons.

Admitting the difficulty of speaking publicly about personal things, Baker said he "was not certain he handled this matter with the grace and understanding that a good father should have." He did some things well, he said, but "could have used the assistance and guidance of those wiser and more experienced in dealing with grief."

Struck by his humility and vulnerability, I was moved by his admission that even those who have access to the halls of greatest power are also at the mercy of the long sit.

Baker continued, "One doesn't simply deal with the situation at hand and then move on. It can take a lifetime of effort to understand its effects on a surviving spouse and, especially, children. You have to work hard to identify and address the ways such a loss changes one's life."

A *lifetime*, he said. Most of us want things worked out by noon.

*

"You can break the gate down while I am trying to get to the latch," my mother told me when I was an adolescent, impatient for life and for the next big adventure. It wasn't a compliment she gave me.

"You'll love those two days of silence," our friends told my husband and me before we left for our eight-day workshop at the Church of the Savior in Washington, DC, "but Jeanie will be back on the first plane!"

Our workshop began with two days of silence and solitude, and what my friends did not know was that God was leading me to a discipline that would transform my life. Instantly, upon entering the silence at the retreat center, I knew that I had found something I had been seeking for my whole life, and while the discipline of being still and waiting was unnatural for my impatient and impulsive self, it was precisely what I needed for balance. It was also preparation for living with the hard and difficult processes of life.

Learning to wait in the silence was one thing. I've had to struggle with my need to control outcomes, my need for results, and my restless body that begins to scream at me as soon as I try to be still and quiet. *This is mind-numbingly boring!* I have said to myself more than once when I have participated in the lengthy "sits" at the Benedictine monastery in Snowmass, Colorado, but always—every single time—I have come away from those eleven-day retreats changed, healed, forgiven, or empowered in some way that is mysterious and amazing to me.

What I have had to learn in waiting through the long and painful processes on the ash heaps of grief and loss of transformation and growth have been quite another kind of learning. There is, however, no real transformation without the waiting process, it seems, and that process cannot be rushed. No step in it can be circumvented. In fact, waiting is a prerequisite for the gifts of the journey.

Transformation takes as long as it takes, and the secret no one tells you on the front end is that you never really do "arrive." Redemption, transformation, and salvation happen over time; in fact, the processes of coming to wholeness require a lifetime.

So it was that our hero Job, now covered with sores, found himself on an ash heap outside the town, stripped of everything that had ever given him meaning and purpose, security and safety, prestige, power, and predictability. Reading the book of Job, you have to marvel at how he was able to tolerate the long sit required of him.

What else could he have done, given the circumstances? He could have picked up and moved, by cover of night, to another place, taken a new name for himself, and started over, I suppose.

On the other hand, he could have stayed right where he was and pretended that nothing had happened. He could have pretended that it didn't hurt, or he could have gathered his friends around him to search out the bad guys who had brought this terrible turn of events on him, blaming and blasting "them" for his losses. If he were living in contemporary culture, he could have sued someone, anyone!

Job could have turned bitter and vengeful; he could have numbed himself or distracted himself from his pain with substances, activities, or persons.

Job could have found any number of ways to avoid the horrors of his losses, including killing himself. He could have found a way out of the terrible process of grief. Life for Job would never be the same, and he was faced with the terrifying process of recovery, and the truth is that recovery is slow. It is difficult, and there are no guarantees. You can know, for sure, that you won't be the same when you come through your ash heap/recovery process, and that it will take far longer than you want it to. What makes Job's story relevant generation after generation is that he chose to go into his pain instead of running away from it.

In the shock of it all, did Job wonder if he had it in him to get through the process? Did Job, like many of us, ask himself if it was worth it?

We don't know if he took himself to the ash heap or if he was taken there, but we do know that the voice of hopelessness and despair came to him through his wife.

"Curse God, and die!" she told him, and we have to remember that she, too, had lost everything and was in the grips of grief and confusion.

It was an easy way out that Mrs. Job suggested, a way out of the pain and embarrassment, and a way out of the agonizing, tedious, and sometimes unbearable process that lay ahead. Indeed, when pain is severe, who doesn't want a quick fix, a shortcut, and a palliative?

Far too often, the voices that urge you away from the hard way are the voices of the people closest to us. It was, in fact, Peter, one of Jesus' closest friends and disciples, who urged him not to go back to Jerusalem, where Jesus would surely meet trouble. Jesus' seeming harsh words to Peter, "Get behind me, Satan," are indicative of the seriousness of arguing someone away from what is inevitable and necessary for their healing and transformation.

*

"I'm worried about our friend," a woman told me, referring to a mutual friend whose young husband had died suddenly.

"Why?" I asked. "Has something else happened?"

"It's been *two weeks* since the funeral, and she is still crying! She's not eating, and she's not getting out. Why, she needs to *get over it* and move on with her life!"

Contrary to more primitive cultures that allowed persons a full year to grieve, we "modern" and "sophisticated" people will usually give a person two weeks to grieve. If only we could just get over those deep wounds quickly and easily and move on with our lives, but grief has its own agenda and its own timetable, and the way to ensure that it will last forever is to try to rush through it.

Several years ago, the long-anticipated birth of the baby of one of my dearest friends, Mary Ellen Hartje, led her to an ash heap she had never anticipated. Her precious baby girl and her third daughter, Erin, was born with Pierre Robin syndrome.

For months, the feeding of that precious little life was tedious and time-consuming. Every feeding for the first nine months of the child's life required at least an hour, and only part of the feeding was successful.

Intending to inquire about the processes leading up to the necessary surgeries Erin would have when she had reached a certain level of maturity, I asked Mary Ellen, "How long are you going to do that?"

There was a moment's silence, as if I had stunned her.

"As long as it takes," she responded quietly and firmly.

In my own discomfort with my friend's trauma, I had badly worded my question. What I really wanted to know was, "When will the surgeries take place?" My friend taught me with her response, a deeply felt response that was born out of her courage in the face of her own fear and heartache. Mary Ellen gave me a line that has sustained me through the long sits of my own life: *Often, in life, you do what you have to do, and you do it for as long as it takes.*

Mary Ellen's strong resolve and the courage and stamina Erin has exhibited in her life speak volumes to me even now. I turn to her wisdom and Erin's perseverance on countless occasions when I am faced with a long and arduous process.

We who live in this contemporary world are accustomed to instant messaging, microwave cooking, and jet travel. We are addicted to quick fixes; we crave the buzz of speed and pride ourselves on how much we can get done in the least amount of time. In general, we are not very good at waiting. The truth is that most of us human beings want to rush through the processes of life to get to the product as quickly as we can.

"I'm scheduling my C-section," the young mother told me. "I can't stand not being in control of my body. Besides, labor just takes too long."

The ash heaps of life bring us to the startling awakening that there is much of life over which we have no control, and sometimes, in the process of rebirth, the wait is agonizingly slow. One of the surest ways to make it last longer is to try to rush through the processes. *Suffering takes as long as it takes.*

*

"You fly right up to the flame," I was told, "and then you fly away. When are you going to stop avoiding the pain and go on into it? You won't know what's there until you go step into the fire."

It was a gorgeous spring day, and I was beginning a new phase of my spiritual journey. All of my adult journey had led me to this process, and I was both excited and anxious. I had no idea what was ahead for me; in fact, if I had known, I probably wouldn't have had the courage to begin, but it was time.

In the moment, I was vaguely aware of what this person was talking about, and, frankly, I was a little insulted. After all, I had worked a Twelve Step program for decades. I'd done a "fearless, searching moral inventory" of my life on four separate occasions! I'd faced my character defects, one by one, and I'd had the courage to "take a Fifth Step," confessing and owning up to my faults and failures with my sponsor in my recovery from codependency.

I have a faint memory of something one of the nuns had said to me when I was in training at the Spiritual Direction Institute. I had felt insulted and defensive then, too, when she said, "Your inner child needs to be healed, Jeanie. That part of you is very wounded."

This time, I knew I had to step up to the challenge, and I had no idea how to do that. There was *one thing* or, perhaps, *several things* I needed to face, and I was scared to death. Later, listening to one of my favorite songs by Garth Brooks, "Standing Outside the Fire," I knew that I was being invited into the refiner's fire: "Life is not tried / it is merely survived / if you're standing outside the fire."

"When people tell me they want to go on a spiritual journey," this director of the soul's journey remarked, "I tremble. I don't romanticize this process. All I can say is that you'd better buckle your seatbelt."

How hard could it be? I wondered, excited about what was ahead for me. I wasn't exactly a novice at self-examination, but just as I began to feel the excitement of the journey, that inner voice that always tells the truth said, "If you do this, nothing will ever be the same for you."

I remember stepping outside into the clear, spring day, and it was as if the world stood still. I knew that I had no choice but to step into the fire. I had been brought to it by my choices and by others' choices that had impinged upon my life, and now I'd been challenged. Consciously, I made a choice; I would step into the fire.

However Job got to the ash heap, that place and the long sit there were, for him, his refining fire. It was there, in the agony and the heat of self-reflection and self-examination, that he was to be transformed and redeemed, but, going into it, he had no way of knowing what was ahead or how things would unfold.

*

And so Job sat and waited, but his waiting was not slumber, and it wasn't passivity. It was the waiting of the barren winter and fallow ground, of trees without leaves and buds still locked in seeds and bulbs, waiting for the right conditions to bring forth a crop or leaves, blossoms or fruit. It was the waiting of pregnancy, where you cannot see what is happening, a waiting in which much is going on in the secret and hidden places, protected from the outer world until the fullness of time has come.

Job's was the waiting for life, knowing that in the ways of nature, anything, including death, can happen, but you trust the process. Job's waiting was productive suffering, like the suffering of labor when you know that you trust that what you are doing is, in fact, bringing forth life.

I wonder if Job thought he was going to the ash heap to die, and did he care whether he lived or died? Was he overwhelmed with feelings and sometimes flooded with memories all at once, or did things come to him, bit by painful bit, as he could stand it? Did he cry and wail? Did he suffer in silence, except for his conversations with his friends? How did he manage the despair in the dark of the night? Was there anyone there to bring him food or a cup of water?

"I thought I was through this," I gasped, sitting on the side of a mountain on a perfect Colorado day in August, a full eight months after my father had died. Memories, feelings, suppressed grief, and nostalgia had washed over me, triggered by the presence of old friends and the preparations of a "car mitzvah" for my youngest daughter on her sixteenth birthday. There was something about being away from home that had brought the flooding of tears.

I had led workshops for hospice on the stages of grief. I had sat with countless friends through their own grief experiences, but my father's death was my first encounter with the Grim Reaper, up close and personal, and I'd thought that since I knew so much about death and dying, I could outsmart the grief process. What I was to find out was that the knowing about grief was not the same as grieving; in fact, all of my knowledge was a defense against the pain of grief.

In my own experience of death and loss, I have noticed that death is like a gray monster that grabs you when you least expect it, jerking you around, twirling and tossing you upside down, forcing you to dance at his pace and rhythm, and to unfamiliar music, and he won't let you go until he decides to let you go.

Finally, no matter how much you know, every one of us comes to a place of having to face some cold, hard realities about life and losing: *This isn't going to go away. It's going to take a long time to get over it. I don't know what to do. Nothing feels right. No matter how I distract myself, I always come back to the pain. No one can do this for me.*

"What can I *do*?" I wailed. "Surely I can do something to make this pain go away!"

Be, Jeanie. Just be, came the voice of wisdom.

*

I thought I might die, *just being*, but the truth was that I knew that my addiction to *doing something* to avoid going into my pain was part of my problem, and so I would take a deep breath, cry some more, and start all over, practicing *being*.

The truth is that the more resources a person has, whether intellectual, financial, or relational, the more ways that person can distract himself from his pain and avoid the terrifying leaps into the darkness. The more you are able to buy your way to another vacation, purchase another painkiller of one kind or another, plan another party, or take another seminar, the less you will be inclined to take the long sit on the ash heap.

However, choosing to wait consciously and to go into the discomfort and despair head-on can signal to God and to the pain that you are ready to let the pain do its work with you.

There are ways to survive the long sit on the ash heap, and there are all kinds of people who are available for support for the long sit, people who are much more equipped than Job's friends were to deal with the pain of another's process of suffering.

When you are on the ash heap, find the help you need. It's really unfair to burden your family members, who may also be affected by your long sit, with your "stuff," and so it is healthy and helpful to find a person who is equipped to handle your pain and objective enough to aid you in getting healthy.

"Analysis and self-awareness are not acts of selfishness or narcissism," according to Dr. Jim Hollis. "In fact, it really is an act of kindness and a moral obligation to clean and clear up your inner world so that you will not project out onto your friends and family the toxic waste of your own inner life."

A trained counselor, a depth analyst, a spiritual director, a priest or pastor who is trained to help is invaluable when you are on the ash heap.

*

"I feel as if I am Lazarus, in the tomb," I said when I began my journey of depth analysis. "I can hear Jesus calling my name and telling me to come out," I continued, "but I need someone who can unwrap the death wrappings, someone who can stand the stench." "I can stand it," came the voice of compassion, empathy and uncommon patience.

So I began my long sit on the ash heap. I entered into that cloud of unknowing, not sure of where I was going, but knowing that I could not return to where I had been. I chose, on that day, to allow the spirit of the

Living God to begin undoing the chains of my false self so that the true self, the *imago dei* within me, could be released.

"If you start a process of depth analysis," Dr. Jim Hollis says repeatedly, "you are signing up for an average of six to ten years of the hardest work you'll ever do. Who wants to do that?"

Indeed, depth analysis is often much slower than cognitive or behavioral therapy, both of which have their place. Discovering what lies beneath the surface of your conscious mind sometimes takes longer than you think you can stand, but the truth is that recovery is a lifelong process.

When you take the First Step in Alcoholics Anonymous or any of the other recovery programs, it is clear that the process is for the *rest of your life*. It takes a long time—a lifetime, in fact—to become who you have forgotten to be, the person you were created to be.

Whatever path you choose for doing your own inner work, countless others have found the following suggestions to be helpful in the process:

- Make a decision to work the program fully.
- Choose a healthy sponsor.
- Attend the meetings, and make a commitment to wring the blessing out of the pain of addiction.
- Go boldly into the Fourth Step, taking a "searching and fearless moral inventory," committing to telling yourself the whole, unvarnished truth about yourself.
- Make a decision to do the inner work necessary for transformation. Jesus talked about the kingdom that is within, and it is at the inner part of our being where the real work is done. Accessing what are the inner, hidden motivations, facing the darkness, the demons, the character defects that make you do the things you do is one of the most liberating and transforming processes available to human beings.
- Pay attention to your dreams. Write them down and talk them over with someone who is trained to see the unconscious meaning of dreams' symbols and images.
- Notice your first waking thoughts of the morning, for it is often those earliest thoughts, which arise when your mind is not yet taken over by the ego and your defenses, that contain the deepest truth.
- Look at your physical symptoms, the troubling patterns in relationships, the repetitive patterns that keep on showing up to sabotage your well-being or serenity.

- Pay attention to the times you feel alive and are thriving, and especially notice when you feel drained or lifeless, and ask yourself what the meaning is in your responses.
- Make a commitment to feeling your feelings, all of them.
- Keep a journal. Let go of all your feelings, frustrations, fears, and failures in the safety of your own writings. Then, at the end of the month or the end of the process, discard what you have written as a further sign of letting go.

*

On a hot August morning in 2004, I could hardly wait to get to the hospital to hold my brand new granddaughter, Madeleine. Finally, after her mother had labored for two long days, she was born. We were exhausted, but exhilarated. Her new life signaled a new beginning for us after a series of losses and deaths, and in only five weeks, she was to be joined by two cousins, one born to each of my other daughters. It was an intense time of new life in our family.

Just as I was about to go to the hospital to be with Julie, my daughter, I received a telephone call from a woman, informing me that Scotty Caven, the bright and beloved son of my friend Vivien, had been killed on Interstate 10, on his way back to Houston from the University of Texas in Austin. The news was like a kick in my stomach, and over the next months I witnessed the terrible ordeal of grieving that accompanies the loss of someone who is too young to die.

Over lunch one day, Scotty's mother told me of another mother who had experienced the same kind of devastating loss. This mother had come immediately to Vivien's house following Scotty's death. "This is what you must do to get through this," the woman told Vivien. And then she laid out a plan for surviving what has to be one of the worst losses a person can experience, the loss of one's child.

The counsel she gave is worthwhile, whether you are forced to the ash heap or choose to go there.

- Get enough rest. Grief work and soul work are hard, tedious, and exhausting.
- Get regular exercise and fresh air. Both build energy.
- Pay attention to your nutrition. Eat what will give you life.
- Be with the kinds of people who are supportive of life and of you.
- Minimize your engagement with people who sap your energy.
- Read material that inspires and instructs.

• Get enough solitude to get acquainted with yourself.
• Have an emergency plan and persons to call if you find yourself needing a friend or a friendly voice.
• If you are a giver, make a conscious decision to learn to receive.
• Set healthy boundaries, especially with the people closest to you.

*

"I am 100 percent responsible for myself," a recovering alcoholic told me recently. A magnificent human being, she struggles every day with the burden of depression, a condition that often partners with addictions of one kind or another. "I am responsible for my sobriety, and I am the only one responsible for it. I am responsible for my mental, emotional, physical, and spiritual well-being, and I must act daily to take care of myself."

On the ash heap, we either learn that lesson or we fail one of the tasks of our suffering, and that is the task of growing up and becoming responsible.

Caught in a Job experience, you can make the choice to go fully into the pain and wrest the meaning from it. You can choose processes that will support your own recovery, your healing and liberation, your transformation and your empowerment to live a more free and abundant life. You can choose redemptive suffering, but know that it is costly and time-consuming. It will require a sacrifice, and you don't know, going into it, what will be asked of you.

*

Several years ago, my sister introduced me to Raku pottery. She told me that in this particular form, the potter places the clay piece in the kiln with natural material such as wood, straw, or paper around it and turns the heat up to an extreme level. When the piece comes out of the fire, it is glowing, red-hot, with the heat, and when it cools, it is covered with ash. The potter must then begin the process of scraping away the ash. The potter, having surrendered his work of art to the heat of the fire, doesn't know what color, sheen, or design will appear as he scrapes and shines the piece, but the more he works, scraping and polishing, the more it shines. Our suffering is the fire, and when we enter into it, our outer defenses and our old ego are burned away.

We are never the same, after a long sit on an ash heap. We don't know how we will be changed. We don't even know if we can withstand the heat, and we are, in the process, required to do the hard work of peeling back the layers of ash, the ego structures and defenses that no longer work for us, so that the true self can be revealed.

"Get the lesson in this," I often say to people who come to me for spiritual direction. "Stay in the pain and find the meaning in it so that you won't have to keep repeating the lesson. Don't stop until you wrest the pearl from the pain."

You have to stay in it until you get out of it what is in it, or when you get out of it, you will get right back in it.

Oh, God—I cannot do this.
      I cannot bear this pain.
      You have to take it away.

Give me something, anything.
Make it stop hurting.
Make the pain go away. Now.
How long do you think
I can stand this?

What do you think I'm made of?
Do you not know
      that this is unbearable for me,
that you have left me
in this so long
that I am weak and worn out
      and I cannot face another day
of this
pain?

I've tried to outrun it.
I've stayed busy.

I've tried to outsmart it.
I've read all about it.

I've distracted myself,
medicated myself. Oh, God,
the things I have done to

get through this—and where are you,
>   by the way?
And what are you doing while
>   I sit here, bent double
in this long,
dark
night
that will
not
end?

>   You call yourself the Great Physician.
>   You've even said that you are the Comforter.
And you promised you would not leave me . . . or forsake me.

So where are you now? And what are you up to?

Chapter Five

The Friend Problem

*When pain is to be borne, a little courage helps more than much
knowledge, a little human sympathy more than much courage, and the
least tincture of the love of God more than all.*
—C. S. LEWIS

*I do not envy people who have never known any pain,
physical or spiritual, because I strongly suspect that the capacity f
or pain and the capacity for joy are equal. Only those who have
suffered great pain are able to know equally great joy. Suffering
leads us to the heart of God, opens before us the grace of God
and presents to us compassion for others.*
—MADELEINE L'ENGLE

"I appreciate people's efforts, and I'm sure they mean well," the young
woman, newly divorced, said to me, "but people say things that don't help!"

"Her story is not my story," she continued, telling me about a mutual
friend who had tried to "help" by sharing her own experience. "I know she is
trying to relate to me and that she thinks that hearing her story will help me,
but it doesn't!"

Sometimes well-meaning people add insult to injury by the things they
say, but it's also true that when a person is in pain, words sting in ways that
would, otherwise, roll off your back. The trouble with pain is that it can
make you self-absorbed.

Indeed, it is rare to find a friend who knows what to say when you're hurting. So often, the best intentions end up coming out as platitudes or bromides that leave the hurting person feeling as if he is weird of flawed or guilty for having the problem.

"I'm finding that I can't talk with my old friends without being angry," my longtime friend told me after the tragic death of her thirty-one-year-old daughter.

Well, of course you feel angry when your precious child has been snatched away from you and your friends try to comfort you or, worse, try to act as if they really do understand when the truth is that every single loss and every grief experience has its own unique agony to it. While there may be a "typical" pattern to the grief process, every person experiences his loss in his own way, and the process of grieving is a profoundly individual process.

"People who have lost a child tell me that they know how I feel," another grieving parent told me, "but they didn't lose Benjamin! No one could possibly understand what it is like to lose that kind of son!"

Sometimes the pain is so great that you don't even hear what you are saying and you forget that other people's losses are as great for them as your own.

No one can fully be inside the mind and heart of another person, and while it is, in certain circumstances and with some people, helpful to be around people who have experienced a similar loss, each person who is grieving experiences his own process in his own unique way. To each person, his own grief is profoundly distinctive and the loved one distinctively special.

The reality is that tragedy and catastrophe change you, and they change everything about your life, including how you feel with your old friends and how you feel about yourself in what used to be your "life." When trouble hits, everything that used to be is forever changed, and what is changed most profoundly is your own way of being in the world!

It is appropriate that the process Job was to go through was set in the context of intense conversations with friends because friendship is a motif in Oriental literature. What better way for Job to work out his trouble than in the presence of trusted friends and in conversation about his trouble? What greater antidote for his pain and suffering than the presence of friends with whom he had history? Who can comfort us more than the people who know us best?

Well, sometimes that friendship thing turns out well, and sometimes tragedy has a way of slicing through the relationships of our lives, separating out who really is a friend and who isn't. Sometimes our friends can't take our suffering and they leave, and sometimes they do the wrong thing and we can't take them! Sometimes trouble exposes the fault lines of the relationships, flaws in the friendship that have been there all along, but, in the face of hardship, make the friendship collapse on itself.

You have to give Job's friends some credit. At least they made the trip to see their friend. At least they took the trouble even to go out to the edge of town and to the ash heap. That couldn't have been easy for any of them. After all, they were accustomed to relating to their friend as the successful and respected leader that he was, and it had to be hard on them to see Job, stripped of everything, naked and covered with sores, out on the outskirts of town, humiliated and broken. And it had to have been hard for Job to be seen by his friends in such a condition. That ash heap of sorrow would take each of them to the edges of their own concepts of God and suffering.

Did Job, I wonder, fear their pity? Was he humiliated in front of them, or was his pain so great that he was beyond feeling humiliation? Was Job embarrassed, ashamed, or so ravaged by his losses that he could no longer care what others thought?

Was he afraid that they would withdraw from him in revulsion? Would they talk about him to their other friends? Would they think less of him, now that he was humiliated and stripped to his sores? Did he wonder if they could handle the extent of his suffering? Would they blame him for his own troubles?

Did Job scramble for some kind of covering to protect himself from their scrutiny? Did he hate for them to have to endure such a sight?

Eliphaz, Bildad, and Zophar each traveled from his own country, going together to see their friend Job and to comfort him, and when they saw him, the sight was so horrible that all they could do was cry out in lament, tear their robes, and then sit with him on the ground in utter silence for seven days and nights.

"There are no words that will comfort you," a wise person told a grieving man, "but I will sit here with you. I will be here for you. I will listen to you if you want to talk, and I will be quiet when you want to sit in silence. I am not afraid of your grief."

For me, presence is what I need when I am hurting, but it is presence that respects my privacy and is sensitive to boundaries.

*

My father used to tell a story about a little girl, Janie, who ran home from school, burst in the door, and told her mother that her friend's mother had died. The wise mother took time to sit down and talk with her young daughter about what that would mean for the little girl, whose name was Molly.

In the next few days, Janie reported each day that Molly had not yet come back to school, and she wondered aloud how it would be when she did come back. Janie's mother allowed the child to express her own anxiety, but she assured her daughter that she would know what to do when Molly did return to school.

In a couple of weeks, Janie came home and reported that Molly had, that day, returned to school, and that it was a hard day for everyone.

"Mom, Molly put her head down on her desk and cried," Janie said, tearing up.

"And what did you do?" the child's mother asked, taking her own child in her arms.

Through her tears, Janie answered, "I sat down beside her and put my head down and cried with her. That's all I could do."

And that was enough.

*

When I have experienced a shock or a loss, I've wanted some time to myself to pull myself together. It's bad enough to be suffering, but to be scrutinized (Is she holding up?) or evaluated (How bad is it?) or judged (She should have known this was coming!) is difficult for me. I prefer to have my worst moments by myself or with only the people who are closest to me.

When my defenses have been stripped away and I feel exposed and vulnerable because of what has happened in my life, I need time alone to pull myself together.

Job's nakedness stands as a symbol of being brought to the point of extreme vulnerability without the "coverings" of defenses and masks that typically hide our pain and our shame. His agony was out there for anyone and everyone to see and scrutinize.

Some people are more open about their suffering and more willing to suffer in front of others. Some people are comfortable, in their most private agony, being around others, and some crave the presence of others.

Because of my life history, I have been with many people in those shocking moments when loss is fresh and raw and terrible, and I am often surprised by the various responses to loss. I have vivid memories of strong, confident men being brought to their knees by the ravages of grief and wailing, uninhibited and spontaneous. I have seen people who are emotionally expressive suddenly find a center of calm and composure within themselves at the moment of crisis.

There are those, as well, who enjoy the attention of others and are prone to make the most of their bad times. Some even use their wounds or sorrows to punish others, almost using their "sores," either literal or figurative, as weapons to say, "See what you did to me?" or "See how hard I have it?"

We don't know what Job was feeling about being seen in his condition, but we do know that he did not make any attempt to hide any of the ugliness of his condition behind any kind of façade. Whether he was too sick or too weak to cover his agony, or whether he was embarrassed or ashamed, he was transparent and completely "out there" with his condition. For Job, this was no time for pride or false modesty. In contemporary terms, his vulnerability was a bold statement that said, "It is what it is."

*

"What will people think?" was a guiding principle of my childhood, and it took years of maturing for me to get over my concern with what people would think. Finally, I woke up to the startling fact that people were, in general, thinking about themselves and what was going on in their own lives!

It also occurred to me, on a bright spring day, that I was caring more about what *others* thought about what I was doing than *I* thought about what I was doing! I realized that in concerning myself with what others might or might not be thinking, I was handing over the authority for my life to other people, some of whom I hardly knew! Sometimes I was in an emotional knot over the opinions of people who weren't really in my "inner circle of concern."

The truth is that people are going to think what they are going to think and they are going to talk. People will draw conclusions based on their own experiences and biases, and they will project their own experience onto yours. Some will judge you, and others will have mercy; some will blame you, and some will exonerate you. There are those who are leaping for the chance to nail you with guilt, and others who won't believe the worst about you if it's staring them in the face. Soon, however, you will be old news; as Elizabeth Taylor observed, "Today's tabloids will be on the bottom of the bird cages tomorrow!"

Nevertheless, when tragedy strikes, you are different, and how you are with others is going to change. Some relationships are changed instantly; with others, it takes some time to see if the relationship can survive the trauma of tragedy.

Surely, in those seven days of silence, all kinds of thoughts and disturbing questions were churning in the heads of Job and his friends as each of them processed, in his own way, the reality of Job's condition. In those seven days, each had to come to terms with the fact that what had happened to Job was challenging everything they had experienced in the friendship that used to be. The bad news of Job's life was changing the dynamics of their interactions forever, but one thing seems clear: Job's battle did not seem to be about what people thought; instead, it was a fierce and mighty struggle with the Almighty.

In truth, all our major struggles are, at their core, struggles with God, and if we can work those out, other things tend to go better.

*

"You know that we don't expect all the news to be good news," a mother had to say to her adult child, who had been hiding the news of his business failure from his parents. "We can handle this, and we can help you handle it, but we can't handle it if we don't know the truth."

"I know, Mom," the son responded. "I just couldn't stand for you to see me in this condition. I knew it would hurt you, and I didn't want to hurt you."

"I just dread telling my children what the doctor said," a parent told me. "I hate for them to have to see me suffer. I hate the way my illness is going to inconvenience them. I don't want them to have the expense of having to care for me. And I hate knowing that I'm going to die and they are going to be alone."

Indeed, loving others and living in family and being together through life exposes us to the pain and the loss of each other. To love is to take a risk; at some point, someone is going to have to let go of the other. We expose each other to all kinds of suffering when we choose to form relationships, and that is part of the burden of being human and having the capacity to love and to feel.

Job needed the presence of his friends, and they did give him that. Unfortunately, however, they also gave him more. It is about friends like Job's that one can surely say, "With friends like these, who needs enemies?"

One by one, beginning with Eliphaz, the friends began to speak to Job about his condition, accusing him of some unconfessed sin, challenging him to own up to his dark deed and be done with whatever had landed him on the ash heap. Each friend took his turn, and then two more (in what are called "discourses" but appear to me to be more like lectures), hammering away at Job because they didn't know what else to do in the presence of such agony.

To Job's credit, he stood his ground, however weak he was, against his friends' assaults on his character and his relationship with God. Something big was brewing within Job, and he would not let his friends' diatribes shake his encounter with the Mystery.

Job's friends were speaking from what they knew about God and from what they had experienced in the past, but for Job all of the old ways were gone forever. What they offered Job was all they knew to offer him, but he could not accept it because his tragedies had put him on a fast track to internal change. If he had listened to his friends, Job would have stayed stuck in his suffering and we probably would not have heard anything about him.

One of the things that makes the story of Job compelling is that God had led Job out on the edge of his understanding. Job was disoriented and confused; he was disturbed and in the depths of despair, but he was being led into a new place, a place he'd never expected to go. Job's suffering was changing him from the inside out, and in psychological terms, he was being thrust, pushed, propelled, and throttled into the process of individuation, the process of becoming one's own true self.

*

It's easy to disdain and censure the friends of Job and to decry their tactics, and all of us can point to times when we have been the victim of someone's faltering and bumbling attempts to "help."

"He means well," people will say when someone does something that hurts instead of helps, and that is a gracious band-aid to put over a misspoken word or deed. However, in this era of communication training and in a time when the processes of grieving are easily available, it is possible to learn what to do and what not to do when you talk to someone who is hurting. In today's world, there's not much excuse for not knowing what to do or say when somebody's life has just been torched by a Job experience. "Meaning well" is no excuse for messing up.

Perhaps, however, for those of us who want to glean the fullness of the Job story for our own lives, it is helpful to consider the friends in the story not as external to him, or to our own suffering, but as part of the inner voices and inner complexes that attack and accuse us when we are hurting.

I sabotage myself.

I am my own worst enemy.

When I mess up, I beat myself up. No one can make me feel worse about what I've done. I don't let up until I've thoroughly whipped myself, verbally, with all the accusations about what I should have done that I did not do, and what I did that I should not have done.

Interpreted as an inner dialogue, Job's "discourses" could be his own self-examination. The voices in those discourses could be seen as Job's arguing with himself, wrestling with his own inner demons, his own belief system, his old prejudices and biases, and his old understanding of God, a wrestling that was necessary and vital for anyone whose life has exploded in his face.

When trouble hits, the loser looks out the window for someone to blame, but the winner looks in the mirror and takes 100 percent responsibility for his part of the problem.

*

In "taking a Fourth Step" in any recovery program, the point of the process is to take full responsibility for one's own addictions, behaviors, and character defects. A wise man told me, "Children blame, but adults take responsibility."

Whether Job's discourses were conducted with actual friends who didn't act very friendly or with his own inner voices, the conversations, as painful as they were, moved Job along the path of his own process, and so we learn from Job's friend problem.

Perhaps, in the big picture, Job's friends served a useful purpose. Perhaps they held out the system of belief that had shaped Job's early life so that he could argue with it.

Perhaps the friends articulated in full detail the religious system that had shaped and formed Job's faith so he could see that he had outgrown it and that it no longer served him. Maybe the arguments of the friends showed Job the utter inadequacy of his belief system, and perhaps it was because he had been so completely sold out to that religious system that their expressions had to be tough enough for him to see that following the rules and working for external results had led him as far as he could go. Perhaps he had to hear what he did not any longer believe or what was no longer true for him in order to know what he did believe and what was really true.

Looking at the friends through the eyes of understanding and curiosity, you have to see that, in fact, they served a most useful purpose.

A real friend is present when you're hurting and does not abandon you when times get hard.

A real friend knows when to be quiet and when to speak.

A real friend is not afraid to tell you the truth, is not afraid to argue with you, and is not afraid to make you mad.

A real friend doesn't attempt to do for you what you must do for yourself.

A real friend strikes a balance between knowing when to help and when to back off.

A real friend allows you to suffer and respects your suffering.

A real friend does not offer simple answers for complex problems.

A real friend allows you to wail and wallow, but knows when to say, "Enough!"

A real friend doesn't hold you to your failures.

A real friend will wrestle with you through the complex layers of your pain.

A real friend cries with you and celebrates with you. A person who will do one but not the other is not a real friend.

A real friend knows when to challenge you and when to console you.

*

Job was changed by his tragedies, but he was also changed by the conversations with his friends, as painful as they were. In the mysterious ways of God, it was the very difficulty of those conversations that moved Job toward redemption.

I don't know how long Job's friends talked to him after their seven days of silence, but there are three rounds of dialogue in which each of the three friends spoke to Job about his situation. Each of them was coming from his own perspective and from his own prejudices and biases, and each of them, by holding up only a portion of truth or what was no longer true, served an incredibly important purpose of making Job think. By pushing their points of view so forcefully onto Job's experience, they backed him into a figurative corner, forcing him to come face-to-face with a new understanding of God and a deeper clarity about the reality of wisdom.

*

Confronted by a new situation, it is a common thing for us to look for what is familiar and comfortable, as if we are grasping for a firm place to stand. In a foreign country, we seek out familiar words so that we can find our way around. In a new relationship, we are, consciously and unconsciously, asking, "Who is the person like?" In different circumstances, we ask the question, "When have I been here before?" so that we will feel secure and confident.

Eliphaz, the first to speak and probably the oldest, fell into that common trap of "trusting in his own understanding." He had experienced life and God in one particular way; therefore, he thought, what he had learned about life was surely applicable to the life of Job! He had figured out

71

God for himself, and if Job would listen to him, the answers and solutions that had worked for him would surely work for Job!

Eliphaz was full of advice to Job that came straight from his own observations about how God works and how God has worked in the past, and while there is something to be said about one's own personal testimony of his experience with God, people often project their own stuff onto the experience of another person.

*

"I pray to *my* God," the woman told me. "*My* God and I are a majority!"

I could hardly listen for wondering about this personal deity. Realizing that it was all about semantics, I did, however, wonder if she carried around her god in her purse or her pocket, and if she would share it with anyone else!

The woman's heavy makeup seemed to me to be hiding something, and her anxious voice belied her bravado. She and I were struggling to establish common ground in an hour of spiritual direction, and no matter what I suggested, her defenses were solidified around keeping her God behaving in the ways that he had always behaved before. She was so committed to her past experience and so dependent upon God's performing the same way all the time that she could not recognize the fresh breezes that were blowing in the lives of her children.

I wouldn't have understood her so well if I, too, had not had that experience of clinging to my old images and ideas of how God would treat me, but life had pried my hands away from those limited and limiting images in ways that I'd never expected, teaching me step by painful step that the only way we ever grow to a new level of faith is when the current place we are with God is challenged and confronted, often by pain, but sometimes by the invitation to expand our minds and hearts.

God is infinitely creative, and God is always out in the forefront, calling us forward into life, and Job, in his pain, had a sense of that. Job knew that his experience was different from that of Eliphaz, and yet how difficult it must have been for Job to sit strong with the barrage of words and seemingly sound arguments from his old friend!

"It's pretty easy," my father used to say, "to know how another person should manage his time and his troubles."

Bildad's position is much the same as Eliphaz's, but his approach is slightly different, as if he is angry. He has relied on the religious teachings that have been handed down to him, and he cannot endure the irreverence with which Job has spoken.

"I'm not opposed to this change," a bright, successful person told a church leader who was attempting to move the church forward into the twenty-first century. "Theologically, I can't argue with this, but our parents worked things out this way, and I don't want to dishonor them by changing the policies they wrote!"

Bildad comes across as nervous and impulsive. His religious feelings have been hurt, and so he is posing as God's champion. He has been perfectly willing to rely on the ones who had figured out God before him. He had no need to grapple with deep, hard questions on his own, but was content to rest in platitudes and bromides, but God would not let Job buy what Bildad was selling.

When you meet trouble with truisms, you create more trouble. When you attempt to explain Mystery and the mysterious with platitudes, God protests. And when you romanticize the past or concretize what former generations had formalized, you reduce God to a puppet in your own mind, and God will not stand for it.

Bildad may have the right words, and he may know the creed, but it is obvious that he has not had a direct experience with the Living God.

Zophar separates himself from the suffering of his friend by distancing himself from wisdom. It is almost as if he says, "We common folks don't need to mess with these issues." Or, perhaps, Zophar knows that he is in over his head and just does not know what to say.

*

"I don't like to think this deeply," a person told me, and so we returned to our superficial conversations.

"This is too complicated," I've been told by students. "Why can't you just accept things as they are?"

Sometimes I wish I could.

"You are making things harder than they ought to be," the man said. "Why don't you just trust God?"

"I just like to feel good," a young man told me, explaining his involvement in a new kind of church where there is no mention of suffering, no signs of the cross, and no invitations to sacrifice. "What's wrong with feeling good?"

Nothing, I suppose, as long as life is smooth skating for you.

*

The problem is that the three friends and Job are up against the holy autonomy of God, and they are frightened out of their minds. These fallible human beings are face-to-face with that which they cannot explain. God has thrown them a curve and will not bend to their small images of who he is, and so, in their confrontation with the Mystery, they are confounded, bewildered, and confused, and it is they, and not God, who are ornery, stubborn, and contentious.

I have deep compassion for those friends, bumbling around on the fringes of the ash heap. I, too, am confounded in the presence of Mystery. I, too, am struck dumb in the face of great tragedy, and in that moment when the numinous invades my conscious mind, turning my views upside down and whirling me around and around in the mysteries of holiness, cannot define the ways and the wisdom of God any more than I can fly by myself.

All of us do, in any given moment, the best we can. Rarely do we do the best we know, especially when life has handed us a challenge bigger than we've ever had before.

We cannot hide, however, in our ineptitude in the presence of the autonomy of God, for in every situation, we are invited to grow up and grow into the largeness of the Mystery. The truth is that it is not God who is ornery. It is we who are ornery, and we project that state of being onto the Almighty.

God is, instead, gracious and giving, compassionate and generous, loving and life-giving, mighty and mysterious, constantly extending love, grace, and mercy to us, and when we try to make God other than he is, his holy autonomy feels to us like orneriness.

We cannot change God's nature, but we can be changed by his love for us. We cannot make God conform to our expectations, but we can be molded and shaped by his love for us. We cannot dictate to God what he must do for us. We are not privileged to assign the Almighty to our tasks, but we can open our minds and hearts to the transforming, liberating, and empowering presence of his spirit, working within us, around us, and between us, and in that holy friendship, we will come to know that God is always making things new.

The friends tried to explain God to Job just as we who speak about God are always trying to speak for God. The friends thought that they could define the wisdom of God, but Job was coming to a place of knowing that God alone is the source of wisdom.

Listen to me, God—I need
some kind of covering—a fig leaf, you know—

I can't go out in public
like this.

People will look at me and
know what's happened.

They will talk behind their
hands—
you know how it is, God.
Come on. Help me out here.

Cover up these sores for me.
I can't stand to be so exposed.

I need a little time,
some bigger sunglasses,
a cruise around the world—you know

I could disappear for a few weeks. Getting away from the talk
will make it all better.

I can't stand the pity, God;
I can't stand the stares.

God, the pain is hard enough
without having to deal with
everybody's
talk about the pain.
Does it make them feel better about *their* pain
to talk about *my* pain?
Does it make them   forget about their own failures

when they talk about mine?

I'm all exposed. I can't hide. Where can I go? Surely you
remember how it was when your friends abandoned you.

Chapter Six

The Friends' Problem

*I never saw a man who could not handle another's misfortunes
perfectly like a Christian.*
—ALEXANDER POPE

*It's pretty easy to stand on the outside of someone else's life
and know what he should do about his problems.*
—L. D. BALL

On a sunny December day, I answered the phone, only to hear the devastating news that my longtime friend Dwayne Key was being rushed to St. Luke's Hospital from Nacogdoches, Texas. Suddenly, tragedy crashed into the pre-Christmas festivities, forcing all of us to change our schedules for the next few days.

Looking at my friend, the picture of health, now comatose, pale, and dying, I was horrified and grief-stricken. I could not believe that this was happening to someone so young. I could not wrap my mind around the fact that he was really going to die and leave his wife and children. And I could not let my mind even tiptoe around the possibility that if this could happen to Dwayne, it could also happen to my husband.

I did not want to face any of the horrors of Dwayne's death, and I did not want to see the fear and sadness in the faces of his family, but day after day, I kept watch with Angela and the children until the very end. Later, walking away from the cemetery, I felt I'd entered a new phase of my adult life, and I did not like it. Dwayne Key was the first of our friends to die, and I shed another layer of innocence and youth.

There is no reason to believe that Job's friends made their journey to see their friend with anything other than good intentions and, hopefully, some food sent by their wives. Most likely, they intended to give comfort, but they had no idea what they would encounter or how they would feel when they saw the extent of Job's suffering.

The silence of the friends was as much their own bewilderment as it was compassion, respect, and sympathy, but when they regained their equilibrium, they seem to have felt compelled to fill up the silence with some sort of response. When Job had shown in his lament that he could not give blind acceptance to his circumstances, they were disoriented even more, and so they began to lecture him.

As a person who has struggled with codependency for my entire life, I will say that allowing other people to suffer is one of the most difficult things I have ever had to do. To detach from my loved ones, to stop protecting them, to let go of my need to fix their problems and clean up their messes has been a challenge I have met sometimes, but not easily.

The problem is that no one else can do your suffering for you, and to prevent someone from going into their own pain and working their pain is to get in the way of their process of maturing and to interrupt God's work of transformation.

When someone you love steps into that fire of suffering, however, you don't know how they will be when they come out, and you don't know if they will survive the process. Nor do you know, when someone is going through a major crisis, what your own place with that person will be when the crisis subsides.

Friends have described taking their children to treatment centers for various addictions, and the stories of tough love all have a similar tone.

"When I took my precious daughter to that treatment center, she was so furious with me that she wouldn't speak to me," a friend told me, describing the hell she'd been through, simply getting her daughter to a place where she could begin to get some help.

"I had to leave her there with strangers. Both of us were crying, and I had to drive away without a hug or anything from her and trust that she was going to make it through the long, hard weeks of treatment for her addiction. It was the only hope for her, and her life was on the line, but I thought I would die leaving her there."

78

"Would you prevent your child from maturing?" is the question each of us must ask ourselves sooner or later. "Would you deprive her of the opportunity of transformation, just so you don't have to suffer?"

Looking deeply into my own heart, I know that I would do almost anything to keep my child from suffering, but I also know that the only way a human being can mature is by facing the hard parts of life, going into the pain and working the pain until the pain does become the pearl.

"I wish I could walk along beside you and hold an umbrella over you for the rest of your life," my father used to say, and in his acknowledgement, he expressed both his dread of the storms that would come to his children and the necessity of our going through them.

Job's friends had to have faced the hard reality that Job's situation was much worse than they had expected. They had to have been horrified and fearful to face the fact that if such atrocities could happen to so righteous a man as Job, such suffering might also come to them. They had to have been confused about what they believed about God and their system of reward and punishment, and they surely must have wanted to do something or say something that would make Job's pain go away as quickly as possible.

The truth is that we are affected by the sufferings and hardships of our friends and family members. When a loved one faces a catastrophic illness, *something* is happening to everyone around him. You cannot live in community with others and not be changed by what happens to others!

Often, it is in our attempts to handle anguish that we become almost pitiful and impotent. Often, in our desire to help, we harm. Wanting to reassure our friends, we often make proclamations, offer promises, or proffer reassurances that we cannot support. We speak for God, not knowing what we are talking about, and we attempt to apply simple answers to complex issues out of our own discomfort and sense of ineptness.

And so it was that Job's three friends began to speak in a series of discourses. One would take a turn, and Job would respond, and then the other. Round and round they went, speaking and misspeaking, trying to get Job to see things their way. Their words, in fact, were an attempt to help themselves, for what had happened to Job was a huge problem for them!

When we are confronted by the trouble of another person, we so want to find the reason for it. If only we can explain it by going back in the person's family history—if only we can justify it by pointing out the mistakes those people made—if only we can assign blame somewhere—if only we can rationalize it in some way that makes us more comfortable, we feel more in control of our lives. Intellectualizing another's misfortune somehow helps us keep our distance from the problem, and in some strange way, we seduce ourselves into thinking that if we understand how they got in the mess they are in, we can avoid it.

Eliphaz probably spoke first because he was the oldest. He was tactful and cautious, at first, and probably did not intend to say as much as he did. He starts out slowly, and then, his words hanging like empty balloons in the air, his own feelings come roaring to the surface, and the more Job refused to buy what he was selling, the louder and longer Eliphaz talked.

How often it is that the more a person feels out of control, internally, the more he tries to control his external world. The more a person cannot control his own thoughts, feelings or behaviors, the more he presses down on others, trying to control them! It is an illusion, control, and those who feel anxious and afraid cling more tenaciously to the illusion!

The friends' problem was that they referred Job to the very thing about God that Job was questioning. They told him that he should confess his sin and have patience under affliction, and that God was in control of the world, and so Job should trust God.

Basically, they weren't speaking lies, but they just could not allow themselves to be with Job's pain in a way that was redemptive. They were so threatened that they could not see that when you are in the midst of your anguish, none of the old truisms about God feel true, and the person who is suffering will be plunged even deeper into distress and guilt because she is not feeling how the truisms say she ought to feel.

*

When I was a student at Baylor University, I passed a statue in front of the Armstrong Browning library each time I entered that building for my English classes. Taken from a poem, "Pippa Passes," the statue depicted a young girl, and in carved marble were the lines from Robert Browning's poem: "God's in his heaven / All's right with the world." More than one professor began the semester by referring to that quotation, demanding from the students, most of whom had come from conservative religious homes, if we believed Browning's quote.

The very worst part of Job's suffering is that he had taught and lived according to the beliefs about God that Eliphaz was spouting, and now, by life's happenings, that belief was being severely tested. It is we who get up in front of others and declare God's sovereignty and his unconditional love who often are put to severe tests that reveal whether we really do believe what we say or not. It is often we who presume to speak about God and for God who are challenged by life as to whether we can live what we say.

Eliphaz is almost screaming at Job, "Can't you take your own medicine? Can't you walk your own talk?" when what Job needs is the compassion of a human heart.

Eliphaz lectures him about what is true in absolutely beautiful religious clichés and moral platitudes, so there is no progress made in this argument. Job, at best, doesn't feel better; most likely, he feels worse, and the friend doesn't win any points.

The hardest part is that Job, dazed and trying to find his bearings after his whole life has been shattered, realized that these friends are not friends at all. In fact, they have become adversaries, increasing his pain and anguish.

The friends speak much in order to hold themselves apart from Job's suffering. They come down hard in shaming and guilting their friend, for that makes them feel safer and insulated from his suffering. They presume to talk as if they have the answer, and it must surely make them feel better to think that they do, but the truth is that it is their own fear that makes them talk so much.

Eliphaz keeps on talking and digging himself into a deeper hole when he starts using logic and coming on with that "they that plow iniquity" speech. The truth the friends cannot face is that it is God, not they, who keeps the final books. God is the one who does the final accounting, and sometimes God does things in ways that we do not understand or recognize. Sometimes we don't approve of the way the Sovereign God behaves, and we resist coming up against that sovereignty of his.

A song by Beth Nielson Chapman declares, "Gravity throws all these rules in our way—and sometimes the spirit refuses to play." Indeed, the spirit of God is really adept at great reversals and big surprises.

*

Bildad, posing as God's champion, cannot endure Job's irreverence. As his name suggests, Bildad is "God's darling," and so he must, at all costs, retain that position, no matter how Job's condition challenges him.

Most likely, Bildad is nervous and impulsive, and his religious feelings have been hurt. He is so consumed with how his own feelings have been hurt that he cannot be present to Job's hurts.

To Bildad, a rhetorical question is sufficient to dispose of the mystery of the apparent injustice on the part of the divine. "Does God mess up?" he asks, and one has to wonder, "If you're Job and in the worst pain imaginable, how do you answer such a question?"

The trouble is that when you meet trouble with truism, you create more trouble. Intellectual and philosophical wool-gathering does not heal the wound or palliate the pain. Future relief, telling someone that God will ultimately come through, is not a very potent remedy in present grief. Easy answers in the face of complex questions, no matter how intellectually superior they may sound, fall flat on the wounds of a hurting person.

Bildad's words reflect a common belief that a person can pray hard enough, believe right enough, have enough faith, and achieve his own righteousness, thereby controlling God. It is far better when you don't know what the outcome is going to be or whether a person is going to make it through his painful process, to say, "I do not know," than it is to try to explain away the mysterious ways of God.

Poor Bildad. Like so many religious teachers, he knows all the theories and theologies. He knows the creed and he knows how it ought to be, but he has not had the direct experience with the Living God. Perhaps his inadequacy is what prompts him to become cruel, adding further pain to Job's already unbearable burden.

*

Who hasn't been afflicted by a "friend" who is convinced that he or she is just the one who can get through to someone? The lines are the same, and the intention is to get someone to do what you think they should do!

He'll listen to me!
She won't turn her back on me! I can get through to her!
He won't get away with that with me; I'll keep him there until he sees the light!

What inflation it is to presume that you are the one who can break through the logjam of resistance when someone is in trouble. What an abysmal lack of understanding of God's ways with human beings to presume that you can break through the darkness of a soul's sea journey and get someone to return to his old way of being.

All three friends tried to force Job into a confession of his own hidden sin. All three tried to scare him into that confession by painting a terrifying picture of what will happen if he doesn't comply, overtly playing out the arrogance of a person who thinks he can predict the outcome of another's life and another's choices.

The hard, hard truth for the friends is that they are speaking from the inside of a religious system, trying to hold God in the box of their understanding. They are describing what that religious system requires, and what they are saying *sounds* true, at least for the God of their past experience.

In the eyes and heart of God, however, persons are more important than religious systems, and there is a higher law than the law of right, and that is the law of love. God is at work in the depths of Job's heart and mind to reveal himself in a new way, and the friends are so blinded by their own religious rigidity that they cannot see it. Oddly, the friends are showing their own sin, their deep lack of humility and empathy, before the mighty act of God at work in their friend.

My father used to say that the only exercise some folks get is jumping to conclusions! How much more helpful and appropriate it would have been if the friends could have stepped back and stayed in wonder and awe in the presence of the suffering! How much more helpful it would have been if they could have affirmed that God is at work in all things, attempting to bring about good, and then offered to wait with Job while God unfolded his plan and provisions.

How much more redemptive the friends could have been if they could have started looking for the ways that God was healing and loving Job.

Perhaps the friends would have been instruments of God if they could have fallen on their knees before the suffering of their friend and said, "My Lord and my God is at work here, and surely we are standing on holy ground. Instead of roughing up our wounded friend, it is our job to see what God is going to do!"

*

In the years I have spent listening to others' stories, I have come to know that one of the most important practices and spiritual disciplines I must keep is the practice of self-awareness. Without a keen sense of my own inner workings, my complexes, and my shadow, I am prone to project what I think is going on or what I need onto the other person.

Love asks that I know myself well enough to know the difference between what I need and what another needs. Compassion requires my attending to my own issues so that I cannot be drawn into others' issues, unconscious of what is transpiring between us. Empathy demands that I am able to put aside the rumblings of my own soul long enough to hear clearly those of the other.

My friend Larry Boyd is an attorney who works with clients who have experienced catastrophic accidents. He has seen unspeakable suffering in his relatively short career, and I believe one of the keys to his success is in one of his principle methods in dealing with his clients: "Whenever I'm with a client, I let them be and say whatever they need to be and say. I don't judge them. I don't try to make them feel something they don't feel. Mostly, I just let them express whatever they want to express."

I have been in those situations in which there was nothing I could do to make things better.

I know what it is like to want to do or say the right thing so much that I've wound up doing and saying the wrong thing.

I know what it is like to beat my head against the concrete door of another's defenses, only to wake up, finally, to the realization that I am either not the one to help, or the person doesn't anyone's help, or the timing is wrong.

I know what it is like to pour countless amounts of energy into being present to someone, only to have the person walk away with his bottomless pit of needs still unmet.

I am familiar with the pain of extending myself over and over with another person, only to have them be unable, for whatever reasons, to make the changes necessary for health and wholeness. I have seen people paralyzed by their fears, no matter how much I encouraged and supported them.

Thanks be to God, I also know that glorious moment when soul connects with soul and God mediates healing grace and mercy in the spaces between us, and those moments are sacred and rare. It is in those moments when the words that we say to each other become the bread and wine of the presence of God. In those holy moments, God is at work, moving mysteriously back and forth between us, doing what he wants done.

Oh, God—
I look at my friend,
and I tremble.

How did it come to this?

I feel so afraid,
but I am ashamed that
I am afraid.
> I should be compassionate—
> I should get
over myself . . . but . . .
> could what has happened
to her
> > happen
to me?

Oh, God, it is
so awful—this thing is unthinkable!
It is unbearable, and I feel so helpless,
and
I feel so guilty!
> Here I am, healthy
> and whole—and happy . . .
at least for now—and my friend. . . .
> Oh, God, things will
be
different
from now on—and
> I really liked things
as they were, and I have no idea
> how things will be now that this
has happened.
I shouldn't even think about myself.
> I should just think of my
friend.
> You're going to have to help me, God.

My friend's sorrow is too big for me—and too big for her—and . . . I
don't know what to do now—now that things are never going to be the
same.
> Oh, God, help me be there for her, and be here for me.
> Remove my fear, and give me your compassion.

Chapter Seven

The Pain Problem

There are wounds, and there are wounds. Life is inherently wounding.
—James Hollis

If you truly want to grow as a person and learn, you should realize that the universe has enrolled you in the graduate program of life, called loss.
—Elisabeth Kübler-Ross

Wounds can help us; wounds can hurt us.
—James Hollis

The thing about Texas in the winter is that you never know if you'll have summer, spring, or winter on any given day. Often, in January, when the sky is clear and blue and the sun is just right, it's easy to think that winter has passed and spring has come.

It's as dangerous to presume that winter is over in Texas in January as it is to jump to a quick conclusion that you're done with a problem or finished your grieving just because you think it's time to move on or it's been two weeks since your Job experience reared its head into your daily life.

Indeed, people who get out their spring clothes in January are often huddled in their wool sweaters in February, slogging through rain or defending themselves against icy winds with woolen scarves. There is simply nothing that keeps you more humble before the changing whims of Mother Nature than winter in Texas.

In the same way, pain and grief take as long as they take, and on the very day that you think you are over the suffering, something will spring up in the outer world to touch off another torrent of remembering. About the time you think it is safe to declare yourself free of your ash heap, some voice from your unconscious nudges you from below, begging to be heard and respected. In truth, we leave well enough alone when it is, in fact, well enough.

On one of those balmy, beautiful winter days, I finished a speech on "Letting Go," one of three speeches on "Making Space for Grace" that I had prepared for the Women's Retreat at Laity Lodge, an ecumenical retreat center in the hill country of Texas. I hadn't done much with Job in that speech, but I had alluded to him, and the women knew that I was trying to meet a March deadline on this book.

After the break, I went to the back of the Great Hall to sit beside my friend, Kathleen Niendorff.

Just as I'd gotten settled in my chair and the next speaker was beginning her presentation, Kathleen leaned over to me and said, with great seriousness, "I don't like the book of Job. I just thought I'd tell you that."

I had to chuckle, but then I thought, *And I don't like suffering. I don't like it that innocent people have to hurt. I don't like it that life gets harder for many people, the older they get. I am still stunned and horrified at what human beings must endure, and about the time I think I have seen and heard the worst of stories, life wallops me with another one, and I'm forced, once again, to another aspect of human suffering.*

"Life is simply too much for us," says Dr. James Hollis, "and yet we are obliged to take it on."

Did I come here, or was I pushed here? I ask myself as I grapple with my losses and my own stubborn willfulness.

I made a decision to walk right into my own personal suffering and work my own wounds consciously. At times, the process has been unbearably painful, and at other times, the breakthroughs of grace have been so rich that I've known that the process was worth it. Sometimes it has seemed that I was circling the same issues over and over, and at times I have grown discouraged, for it has seemed that transformation takes so long.

Did I choose to do this hard work, I have wondered, *or did it choose me? Was I chosen for this, by some mysterious force, or am I into some kind of self-punishment? Is what I have experienced in life somehow part of my destiny? Is how I am wired somehow connected with my mission in the time I am here?*

Sitting in the meditation room at the Benedictine retreat center in Snowmass or in my sacred space in my own house, both containers for my process, I have sometimes silently screamed, *I cannot do it anymore!* and yet I return again and again to the practice of Centering Prayer.

Being a results-oriented person, I've grown impatient with the slowness of inner work. I've grown tired of holding the pain. I've given up trying to "hold the tension of the opposites," and then, not knowing a better way, I've taken up the cross of pain again, determined to wait well and wait it out and wait for God to do whatever it is that God wants to do with my pain.

In a recent lecture, Jim Hollis said, "It is often in the places where we get wounded that we become conscious and competent," and then Jim said that we must ask ourselves some questions.

What are the messages that came with these wounds?

What do they make me do?

What do they keep me from doing?

I admire Job so much because he sat it out. I admire Job because he spoke the truth about what he was feeling, no matter how uncomfortable that truth-telling made his friends.

I respect Job because he didn't let his friends talk him out of his own struggle and into their interpretation, just so they would feel better or so that he could get them off his back. I respect Job because he chose to go right into his pain and sit with it until the pain of his life produced the pearl of understanding and transformation. Job did scream out that he wished he had never been born. He lamented that he wished he had died at birth and that he could die now.

I respect Job for enduring the ceaseless yammering of his friends, and I respect him for holding himself in the fiery furnace when it would have been easier to give up and die.

*

Jacob wrestled with the angel and would not let go until the angel blessed him. Jonah wound up in the belly of the whale, and that whale journey is another kind of ash heap. Jesus walked straight into the crucifixion and his own burial, and those times of darkness and death have become symbols for us of that terrible time when we are caught in the cloud of unknowing in our own pain.

Naturally, when something catches you and throws you to the ground, you have to go through a period of shock. You have to regroup, and in the beginning, you are often just taking care of business.

After a time, however, when you realize that you are going to have to endure the pain for a period of time, it is possible to choose to work the pain and to help God help you. It is possible to be conscious and intentional about what you do with what has happened to you, and it helps to remember that you can either work the pain now or later.

I'd wanted to do depth analysis since I was in my twenties, having read the books of the Swiss psychiatrist Paul Tournier and participated in Yokefellow Spiritual Growth Groups, which used the work of Dr. Tournier. As a young woman, I searched the book stacks of the Tom Green County Library, looking for books that referenced Carl Jung. I read the writings of John Sanford, Morton Kelsey, and Robert Johnson, often feeling like the man in the Gospels who asked, "Who will teach me?"

Shortly after my mother died, I took a course, "Jung's Map of the Soul," at the Honors College of the University of Houston, taught by a Jungian analyst who is also an Episcopal priest. One statement he made in that class seemed to fly through the air and lodge itself in my memory. Later, it was that one statement that would motivate me to make one appointment with him.

At the time, I was facing four big problems that I could not solve, and while I have come to call those four problems the "four friends" who took me on my mat to Jesus, at the time I was almost beside myself with fear and anxiety, dread and pain, and no matter what I'd tried, I was not rich enough, cute enough, well connected enough, or ingenious enough to solve my problems, and I was quickly being propelled into a crisis of faith.

Nothing that I had learned was adequate for the level of difficulty I was facing, and after a terrifying dream that woke me up and moved me upright in the night, I made an appointment for one session with the instructor, who was also a Jungian analyst.

I had had a frightening dream, and, of course, the first and most basic principle of dream interpretation is that while the dream may be about that person who is in your dream, you have to assume that the dream is about some aspect of your own life that you haven't been able to face in waking time. The unconscious is highly creative in waiting until you are asleep and your defenses are down to send the Dreammaker with a message from the unconscious. I did not know it at the time, but God was at work, bringing to my conscious mind what was in desperate need of being healed.

On the morning after my dream, I attended a group with wonderful and mature women at the Cenacle Retreat Center, where I had done my training in spiritual direction. As we shared our lives with each other, I shared my dream, and instantly, one of the women said, "You need to address this dream, Jeanie. It is too serious and too deep to ignore. You need to see someone who works with dreams."

I was so troubled by my dream, and I knew that my friend was right in her guidance, and so I got up immediately, leaving that meeting, and went home. As soon as I got home, I called to make an appointment with the instructor who had taught the class I'd taken, assuring the receptionist that I was not in crisis. I fully intended to have one, and only one, appointment.

On that bright April morning, just after Easter, I followed the analyst into his office. To the left, just inside the door, is a tall wooden stand, and on it, a luminous wood carving of a mother, gazing in delight into the face and eyes of her infant.

In the bright morning sunshine of that room, it seemed to me that that carving of mother and child was ablaze with life and light, and even now, the way I remember that moment is that the stand and the carving were standing in the pathway into the room instead of over to the side. It's interesting how the mind can play tricks on you when you think you are awake and conscious!

I was so taken by the carving that I gasped and stopped, putting my hand up to touch the wood.

"That's what we do here," the analyst said, obviously noticing my reaction to the carving.

And, indeed, that was what I was to experience, but I did not know that yet. I was going to have to walk directly into the pain of a lifetime if I wanted to experience that "maternal gaze of delight."

Sitting down, I began recalling the statement that this man had made in class. I gave him a brief account of my three of my four problems, and then I told him my terrible dream.

"I can help you with your dream," the analyst told me, "and I can help you with this problem, but let me ask you a question."

I waited, thinking that I would give the answer and, in a few moments, be out and about, taking care of my life, as usual. I even thought he was going to give me "the answer" that would solve my problem, and I could move on with my life, running my errands, meeting my responsibilities, and fulfilling everyone's expectations for what I should do.

He stunned me, though, with a question that seemed to fly through the air, penetrating my defenses and my heart, all at the same time.

"Why are you committing suicide?" he asked, and I was so stunned I couldn't, in the moment, make what seems now to be the logical and obvious connection between my dream and his question.

"What do you mean?" I asked, stammering. Somehow, in a way I could not yet understand, I felt "found out."

"There are two ways to do it. You can do it all at once, or you can do it in increments," he said.

I could hear my heart pounding, and I thought that, surely, he could as well. I could not respond, and he let the silence do its work.

Surely he saw the impact his words were having on me, for he waited, as if to let what he was saying sink in. At the time, I was so disoriented and stunned that I could only touch the edges of the profundity of his words.

"You know," he said, "getting through life, we often make hard choices, deciding between suicide and homicide. We either live for others, denying our own needs, or we live for ourselves, ignoring the needs of others. You're the kind of person who has chosen suicide over a long time, putting others' opinions first, putting others' needs and agendas before your own."

I remember that he stopped and let that information permeate my pain. The true self who was at the core of who I am, the *imago dei* within me, was all bound up in defenses I had built up over a lifetime, defenses that were like death wrappings. I hadn't grown them because I was bad, but because I was trying to keep myself from feeling the pain that was at the core of my life.

Those death wrappings were habits and behaviors that, I thought, would keep me safe and protect me from any more rejection or abandonment. I did not know at the time, but was to learn that the very behaviors which had protected me for a lifetime had begun to be the very means of keeping me imprisoned, killing my vitality and life force.

My death wrappings were the masks and façades I'd constructed, fig leaves they were, to keep other people from knowing what I was really feeling or who I was. My death wrappings were the roles and projections others had imposed on me through the years, the rules and expectations that I'd picked up from my religious culture, and the self-defeating patterns of relating to others that repeated the original wounding over and over and over again.

I needed someone who could listen to me tell my story in a way that would help me get loose from my story.

I needed someone who was able to ask the questions that would lift the scabs from the wounds, but those questions had to be asked gently enough to keep the wounds from being re-injured again and again.

I needed someone who wasn't afraid to challenge my lies that I thought were the truth, who wasn't disoriented when I became confused and who didn't get bored if I had to tell the same story over and over again.

I needed someone who was not shocked at my story and who did not cast blame on anyone—someone who would not let me slide into excuses and self-justification, but who held my feet to the fire of the pursuit of wholeness and freedom.

I needed someone who would help me become strong enough to take full responsibility for all the choices I'd made in my life, even the ones I'd made before I really knew what I was doing. I needed someone who would continue to say, "Come forth! Come forth!" even when I wanted to run back into the tomb.

I desperately wanted to live. I wanted to live and thrive and love and flourish, and I wanted life enough to go to the ash heap to save my life.

I wanted to live my life, the "one wild and precious life" that the poet Mary Oliver talks about, and I wanted my life so fiercely and ferociously that I was willing to do whatever I had to do to work my pain and to wrestle with God until I'd wrenched the blessing from the burden.

I wanted to live so much that I was willing to go into the white-hot heat of pain and feel it. I was willing to know what I knew, to trust myself and my intuitive hunches, to feel what I felt, and to own what I wanted. I was entering a battle for my very life, and I knew it, and I knew that I could not play around with this dark night of the soul.

I wanted to live so much that I was willing to confront the parts of me that were, in fact, committing suicide and ask the hard questions about what needed to die both in outer patterns and inner beliefs and thought patterns. I wanted to pull my life back from the jaws of others' expectations and reorient my world according to the intention of God, who had designed me. I wanted to live enough to challenge my lifelong ego position and dare to let the true self, the *imago dei* at the core of my being, gain the upper hand over my complexes and my character defects.

I wanted to live enough to sit it out on the ash heap, as long as it took.

*

Never again will I announce that I have "worked through" something and can put it, forever and eternally, aside. Whenever I think that I've "arrived," whatever that means, life has a way of puncturing my inflation and letting me know that, usually, we are always vulnerable to being taken over by the thing we thought we'd solved.

When it comes to the hard, tedious work of becoming conscious and responsible, I take off my shoes, for that process is holy ground.

And so, if you have been taken to the ash heap, or if you've gone there voluntarily, it helps to do so consciously and with all the help and support you can gather for the process. The truth is that no one knows how long you will have to stay in the pain in order to find the meaning in it, integrate it, or come to the place of enduring it. No one can predict what "helps" will come to you in the form of outer world occurrences or just the "right" teachers and helpers to push you on your way. No one, including the most highly trained professional, can know what it will take for transformation to occur.

Job sat it out. He talked it through. He leaned into his pain, all of it, and he refused to take the shortcuts out.

I have learned that every time I avoid going into the pain, the pain intensifies until I finally am forced either to take the journey or to increase the dosage of my treatment of choice for pain control.

I have learned that what my mind cannot handle, it will nearly always hand over to my body, and so I must pay close and tender attention to the signals and symptoms my body tries to give me before those symptoms turn into conditions and illnesses.

I have learned that the true self within me, the part of my being that is connected with God or could even be interpreted as the *imago dei*, the image of God, within me, sometimes sets up crises in my external world to push me into a new level of consciousness or to make me wake up to a problem that will not go away.

I have learned that dreams are purposeful and that the Dreammaker speaks in symbols, trying to get my attention by night and make me pay attention to what my conscious mind won't let me see in the daytime. Sometimes I know what the dream means as soon as I wake up, but usually the dream reveals its meaning to me over time. Often, the dream has more than one interpretation.

I have learned from Job that pain has a message in it, and I can either listen now or listen later, but the pain will not go away until it is faced and worked.

In my journal, I recorded the words of Alan Jones, Dean of Grace Cathedral in San Francisco, as a reminder of the gravity of the journey:

> Our destiny is to be burned by one fire or another, and so be either transfigured or consumed. Our pilgrimage is the drama of this choice. . . . There is no escape from the fire; but we do have a dramatic choice between God's flames and those of our own making. The alternative to God's fire is our own burnout—personally and globally.

Oh, God—
> If I had known that I would have to hurt
like this,
> > I might have skipped this part.

If I had seen what was
ahead,
> I think I would have said, "I pass."

> > And if I had known how
dark night could get,
> how long
pain could last,
> > how silent you
could be,
> I would not
ever
have had the courage to
make this
journey
called life.

> > Do you really think I can keep on going?
> Do you really think I can   stand this?

I look around me, and it seems that
everyone else is getting along pretty well.
> Other people seem to be
handling things better than I do.

And I feel guilty because I can't
get it together.
Get over it.
Get out from under it.
Get with it—
> > Please, God, take this from me.
> But, if you won't, please help me
carry it, help me bear it, help me
stand it . . . one breath at a time.

This cup . . . this cup of suffering . . . please not this . . . not this one . . . not this one.

But, if it is, you have to help me. You have to help me. I cannot do it by myself.

Chapter Eight

The Ornery God

*The Beloved sometimes wants to do us a great favor: Hold us upside
down and shake all the nonsense out.*
—HAFIZ

*Too many prayers fail to reach their mark because people do not pray
with emotional honesty. … If we are angry with God, say so; if we love
him, say so; if we are afraid, bring this into our prayer. Prayer is
relationship with God, and no relationship, certainly not with the
Divine, exists without emotional honesty.*
—JOHN SANFORD

"Doesn't that bother you to call God *ornery*?" the woman asked me, and I
think her lips were pursed as she asked her question. "What do you mean by
that anyway?"

I had to chuckle. Certainly, I don't mean that God is cranky or cantan-
kerous, although he did get a little testy with Adam and Eve about meddling
with his apple trees. I don't mean that God is petulant or irritable, although he
did unleash some interesting weather conditions for Noah and his generation.

I'm not even talking about the wrath of God when I speak of God's
orneriness. Instead, I think that God is ornery in that God seems to be pretty
stubborn in his pursuit of us. He seems to be determined to chase us, hound
of heaven that he is, up and down the pathways of our lives with his
stubborn love, and he doesn't seem to give up on us until he has us where he

wants us, and that is right in the middle of his unconditional, unrelenting, transforming love.

"The Virgin Birth is no problem," I told my husband, coming out of my preparation for teaching some of the stories of the women of the Bible for my Thursday morning Bible study. After reading again, with new eyes, the stories of the ways the children of Israel continued the repetitive pattern of turning away from God, getting into big trouble, and then returning to beg for God's mercy over and over again, I had to say, "The bigger mystery and wonder to me is that God has not given up on us, throughout all of the centuries, for we human beings are so very rebellious."

Every generation seems to get confused in new ways about who God is and who we humans are in relation to God, and yet God continues to pursue us with his love, grace, and mercy.

Every generation tries to trap God in one kind of doctrinal or theological box or another. Every generation tries to outsmart, explain, contain, or define God, and yet God remains Holy Autonomy, still loving us.

Every generation attempts to diminish or reduce God to a size and state that is manageable to our finite minds and shriveled hearts, but somehow God keeps on breaking through our barriers, smashing our idols, and showing us that it is not we who define God, but he who defines us.

Each generation finds new ways to break the natural order of the physical universe. Each generation expands on the ways human beings act out their inhumanity, their negligence, and their cruelty on other humans and on the earth, and yet God keeps the door of his heart open to us. My question, when people ask, "How can God allow such suffering to continue?" is, instead, "How can God put up with the ways we human beings inflict such suffering on each other?"

Individuals continue to go their own way, slipping and sliding into arrogance and hubris. Persons play the role of the prodigal son and the elder brother over and over, and yet the waiting Father's love keeps on drawing his children back home.

God's love really is the love that will not let us go, but we have apparently become so deafened to that language that talking about God's ornery love somehow jars us into an awakening and invites us into a discussion about that fierce, radical, tenacious, and endless love of the Creator for the creatures.

*

I'll admit that it does seem a bit strange to refer to God as ornery, and perhaps it is not so much that God is ornery as it is that we fallible human beings don't know God all that well, and so we are prone to project our own characteristics onto the Almighty. Perhaps what we experience as orneriness is, after all, holiness and autonomy.

Perhaps we wrestle with God most when God insists that we grow up, and that insistence on our maturing and acting as adults is particularly uncomfortable if we are chronologically "adult."

It is an amazing thing to me that the impulse toward growth and development is so strong in human babies. Early on, children take pride in their accomplishments. Healthy children look forward to growing up, to the privileges of later bedtimes, to the increased freedom of adolescence and the opportunity to be on their own.

The problem, I think, is that maturity and freedom demand corresponding responsibility, and that is often what slaps a person in the face. "I didn't know it was going to be like this!" the young adult says when faced with the trappings of adulthood—bills, others' needs, the demands of a boss, the challenges of everyday life.

The process of spiritual growth begins with the dependence of childhood, but must evolve and change so that the person moves to a place of living from within, answering to an inner authority instead of the competing complexity of external authorities.

Traditional religion trains us to rely on the authorities of the leaders, but Job was being called to a new relationship with God, and his experience foreshadows the radical change articulated by Jesus.

"The kingdom of God is within," according to Jesus, and yet the journey of letting go of one's attachment to the outer kingdoms and the demands of those outer voices to a place of obeying the still small voice of God who dwells within the human heart is one fraught with difficulty and peril.

Job, on the ash heap, was being forced to turn away from the voices of his friends, representatives of external authority. He was in an enormous inner battle and was being moved from within so that his locus of personal authority was not in a religious system, a church, or any institution, but was the voice of God, speaking from within his own being.

I admire Job's tenacity in not allowing the friends to force him to make a confession that he did not need to make. I admire his willingness to stand up to them and challenge their positions. As a recovering people-pleaser, I am impressed with his courage and faith in holding his position in the face of their insistence that they are right and he is wrong. As a person who has feared being wrong, I respect the way Job stubbornly holds to the power of his inner experience.

Children must rely on their elders to be safe and to learn how to live in the world. Adolescents and young adults must conform and adapt to the outer structures in order to complete an education, get and keep a job, establish themselves in the community, and get along with peers, teachers, bosses, and supervisors.

Richard Rohr, in his book *Job and the Mystery of Suffering*, says, "Mere trust in outer authority almost always creates fear-based and shame-based people, who easily resort to subterfuge or denial." In fact, it is Job's religious tradition that was the problem, and it is often contemporary religion, either in the current trends of fundamentalism or feel-good religion, that keeps people infantilized and dependent on the institution as a substitute for an authentic relationship with God.

Job reveals to his friends and to us a higher level of maturity, a maturity that is based on personal responsibility, authenticity, and integrity.

There comes a time for all of us when God calls us to grow up, and if we don't get the message one way, God is infinitely persistent in pressing in on us with the invitation to mature into all that we have been made to be. The summons to maturity may come in one of the Job experiences described in the first chapter of this book, or it may come in the inspiration from nature or from a piece of music, a sermon, or an invitation to love. However it comes, the summons to grow up must be taken seriously.

The poet Hafiz, who lived in the fourteenth century, says that we have only two choices about growing up and living the life we are intended to live:

You have been invited to meet
The Friend.
No one can resist a Divine Invitation.
That narrows down all our choices
To just two.
We can come to God
Dressed for Dancing,
Or
Be carried on a stretcher
To God's Ward.

Perhaps our hardest lessons in life are dance lessons, in which we are being taught the intricacies of more interesting dances. Perhaps in our suffering, we are invited into the fullness of life in new ways that we can't even imagine.

God intends to mature us and bring us into the full measure of what we are capable of being.

"You can get the message with a feather," I tell myself and others, "or you can wait for the two-by-four to the head."

The truth is that I much prefer dancing to stretches and feathers to two-by-fours, but often, in my own arrogance, I think I can put off growing up, even now.

*

The ornery God who insists that we grow up also will not let us hide behind the fig leaves of our excuses and our defenses. Eventually, we are brought face-to-face with our own mistakes, our faults and defects, in one way or another, and it is sadly true that what we do not face, our children often must face, paying our dues in ways that hurt and hinder their development.

"Where were you when that was going on?" the victim screams, demanding that God give an account of his presence when bad things happened to innocent children or adults, and the unchanging answer is that God was there, in the middle of the atrocities, attempting to bring about good.

"Why didn't you stop this?" the bereaved sob when that which is most precious is snatched from them, and the silence of God announces his sovereignty, all the time wooing the broken-hearted to go deeper into those hard questions in order to discover that God's ways are not our ways, but that God is still, nevertheless, nearest to the broken-hearted.

"You could do something about this!" we accuse God, trembling in the face of the outcome we cannot bear, and we are met with the majesty of the Sovereign One who meets us at the places where we do not know the answers, where the dots no longer connect, and where it feels that we are stepping out into the dark blackness of the abyss.

God allows us to suffer, for even God conforms to the physical laws he has set in motion. However, even when we give up on God, God seemingly will not leave us alone, and in the midst of our wrestling with God and who God is, we are called to own what belongs to us, but only what belongs to us. We are asked to take responsibility for the mistakes we have made, to make amends, and to attempt to find ways to correct the wrongs we have done, and sometimes we are called upon to face the wounds that others have inflicted on us so that we don't keep on using our own wounds as weapons on others.

"Hurt people hurt people," Jim Nutter, the rector of Palmer Episcopal Church said to us at Laity Lodge. Gathered together for a weekend retreat, we listened intently as Jim described the realities of a wilderness experience.

Indeed, it is street knowledge now. Everyone knows that people who are hurting will hurt other people, but we cannot hide behind that excuse. Once we become aware of what we have done and what we do to hurt other people, we become responsible for changing those behaviors and stopping the cycles of violence, abuse, and misuse of other human beings.

If God seems to be severe, it is because he cannot overstep the boundaries of the wonderful/terrible, gift/burden of free will that God himself has given us, but he does, nevertheless, call to us from the other side of the walls we have erected, the defenses we are maintaining, and the resistance to his love that we hide behind, announcing that he is, no matter what, going to keep on pursuing us until we realize that we have been, all along, right in the center of his presence.

*

If God appears to be ornery and relentless, it is because God is, after all, jealous, and he is jealous because God cannot tolerate our devotion to the lesser gods that diminish, devalue, and devour us, creatures made in the very image of God. Because God knows who we are and how we are made, God knows that our surrender to the lesser gods will lessen us. Our enslavement to the feeble gods will cripple us, preventing us from living up to the high calling of creatures, made just a little lower than the angels.

God is ornery because he insists that we face him and talk to him and with him and not just about him, and it seems to me that we who are a part of the religious establishment who are so fond of talking about God often get some of the most severe tests. God insists on a personal, vital, dynamic love relationship with him. He insists on a "friendship," as Jesus told his disciples, and God pursues us in the midst of our difficulties with an untiring love.

God is ornery because he allows us our regressions and retreats, but is always waiting for us on the other side of them.

Throughout the book of Job, our suffering friend comes to statements of astounding clarity and faith, and then, almost instantly, falls back into a walk in the park of his past, which is now dead, lamenting how things used to be and sometimes wallowing in self-pity.

"You can have one day of self-pity," a friend was told when she entered a treatment center for depression and addiction, following the tragic loss of a family member. "And really do it well, if you're going to do it. Wallow well.

Weep as loudly as you want to. Scream at God. Rail against your fate. Feel all the feelings to their bottom."

My friend said that she was stunned at the permission to "welcome" what she had been trying to press down. All of her friends had tried to cheer her up. Relatives had chastised her for not getting over it and moving on! And her own inner voices had shamed her for feeling the agony and anguish of loss.

"But you only get one day," the counselor said to her. "Then we go to work on recovering."

Whatever else God is and however else God is, God will be true to his essential nature, and that nature is pure love, radical grace, and unmitigated mercy. The thread of redeeming love is woven throughout the entire biblical narrative, and it is that redeeming love that keeps Job wrestling with God. It is that love that will not let Job go that gives him the strength and stamina, in his weakness, to sit it out on the ash heap. It is God's pursuing love that calls out to him, even as Job agonizes over his plight.

I have to confess that I've always been a rebel when it comes to prayer groups. I've tried and tried, through the years, to participate in them, but from the time I was young, I have not been able to conform to the various programs that instruct people in getting God to answer their prayers.

There is something in me that rebels when the focus of prayer meetings is on telling God what to do. Somehow I get restless when we make the announcements from the church calendar or remind God what is going on in our prayers. And I get a little weary of the "organ recitals," when we pray only for the sick, telling God how to heal the various hearts and lungs, and I almost bolt out of the room when we assault the heavens with our own political agenda, announcing how bad our enemies are and how good we are in this "Christian nation."

Don't get me wrong. I do believe in the biblical injunction to bring our requests to God. I do pray for others, and there are times when the little child in me cries out, "Help me!" I do beg God for favors, and I do make suggestions to God about how best to run the world. I pray for my children, and I ask for protection. I pray for forgiveness, and I make my bargains with God. I do all of those things when I'm skating around the edges of praying.

There is something about that kind of praying, however, that runs me straight into that holy autonomy of God that Job faced on the ash heap. There is something about my telling God how to run the universe that sets me up for frustration.

When my oldest daughter was about eight, I had given her some kind of instruction for the afternoon, and as she marched down the hall toward her room, I heard her chanting, "Do this. Do that. That's all she knows how to say. Do this! Do that!"

I can remember how it felt to walk into my house, tired and needing some solace and silence, only to be confronted with the competing demands and needs of three children. Longing for a moment to catch my breath, I had to, instead, try to sort through the needs of my children, assessing which was most urgent, while, at the same time, I was preparing the evening meal.

Now, those same children come to be with me just because they want to spend time with me. They want to visit with me. They want to hear about my world and tell me about theirs, and there is an ease and a delight in being together.

Again, I don't believe that God is a glorified human or a bigger-than-life mother/father, but it does make me understand the nature of prayer and the character of God to recall those times when I felt overwhelmed by the demands of my children. Surely, God must love it when we want to commune with him, just because of the pure pleasure of being together.

*

I've learned a different way of praying, sitting on my own ash heap, and frankly, I don't know if I was pushed and shoved into the realm of contemplative praying, or if I went there voluntarily. Maybe it was a little bit of both, but I do know for sure that learning to practice the presence of Christ, reading the works of the great contemplatives and practicing the sacred discipline of meditation, solitude, and silence and listening prayer with those who know how to be still and know God has changed my life and my way of praying.

It has been through my years of training in Centering Prayer that I have learned that instead of rushing into the presence of God with my own agenda, it is essential that I suspend my need to control outcomes and wrest my will and way from God and learn to simply open my mind and heart to the presence and action of God. In the silence, I have learned that it is much more important for me to listen for the ways and the will of God than it is for me to tell God what to do. It is much more productive for me to wait on God with an inquiring mind than it is for me to inform God of what he can do with my current petitions.

Too often, my prayer requests have my own agenda overlaying the situation. Too much, my own ego needs and selfish desires interfere with the will of God, and it is humbling and sometimes humiliating for me to realize that, often, when I have laid out my perfect plan for God to complete, I have limited God by my own lack of vision or imagination.

Now, more than ever, I increasingly simply hold the need of another or the desire of my own heart in the silence before God, trusting that the One who sees the whole picture and the end from the beginning will act in mercy and in love within the situation. My usual prayer for myself and others is more often, "Thy will be done."

God is concerned about every one of the players in every situation, after all, and is not my own private, personal bellboy. "God is not your Sugar Daddy," proclaims a billboard outside a church near my writing studio.

Indeed. I no longer presume or dare to tell God what to do before I have spent time simply holding my need or the need of another in the silence. If anything, I ask God to show me where he is at work so that I can cooperate with him. Prayer for me now is more about seeking and asking and knocking than it is about telling God how I think he should manage his affairs.

Job and his friends were to come to the jolting knowledge that wisdom is not in science. It is not to be found in religious technique or in knowledge.

God is the source of wisdom and God *is* wisdom, at work in the world, blowing like the wind, where and as God's pleases.

God's unchanging grace is alive and free and constantly at work, and when we try to change God, we are thrown up against that orneriness of God.

You're not giving in, are you, God?
  You've got me
    right where you want me,
  don't you?

Who do you think you are?
  What do you think you're doing with me?

  I don't get it.
  You give us this free will,
and you tell us we can choose.

And so I chose.
I even prayed about it before I
chose,
        but it hasn't turned out like I thought it would.
        It's been so much harder than I would ever have
imagined.
        There's been one
obstacle
after another.
        And I am finding myself
wondering if I
heard you wrong.
        I've heard you are the love
that won't let go.
Is this love?
        I've heard that you will never leave me.
Are you still with me?
If you are, why do I feel so
alone?
        I've heard that you won't give us more than we
can stand.
        Could we talk about that?
Because my view of what I can stand
and yours don't seem to be the same. You win, God.
        You've got me. What now?

Chapter Nine

The False Gods

[God] is the name by which I designate all things which cross
my willful path violently and recklessly, all things which upset
my subjective views, plans and intentions and change the course of
my life for better or worse.
—CARL JUNG

You shall have no other gods before me.
You shall not make graven images.
—GOD

The young woman sat at a darkened bar, alone and tired. She had long fought her addiction to alcohol, but away from home in a city where no one knew her, she had found her way to her favorite place and her drug of choice for numbing the persistent cry of her soul. Having come from a successful meeting with leaders in her chosen field, she sought refuge in the haze of her nightly habit.

Caressing the neck of the green glass bottle, she could see her reflection in the mirror over the bar. Suddenly, looking into that bottle, a voice from within her said, "This isn't nearly a big enough god for someone like you."

She put down the bottle, left the bar, and began a long, laborious, tedious recovery from her addiction to alcohol.

It was Carl Jung who said that addictions were a spiritual problem, and that the only answer for dependence on a substance was "a bigger God."

Job's problem was not a drinking problem. However, an addiction can be defined as an idol or a false god, and human beings have a tendency to turn to substances, behaviors, or persons to assuage and soothe the anxiety of life. Persons make gods out of something outside themselves to manage the rage of emotion and treat the inner turmoil, conscious and unconscious, within them, thereby creating for themselves self-defeating patterns.

*

I sat with my own Twelve Step sponsor, Sandra Hulse, week after week in the same booth at the Crystal Confectionary, a restaurant in San Angelo, Texas. My sponsor is a recovering alcoholic, a black belt sponsor to me, though she had reluctantly agreed to walk me through the Steps. "I don't know if I can do this since you aren't a drunk," she told me, "but I will try."

Periodically, as Sandra listened to me as I tried to work my way through the Steps, she would put her head in her hands and utter a sound of frustration. "If only you were an alcoholic," she would say, lamenting my halting steps and my stubborn resistance. "Until you get *people* off the throne of your life, you won't get anywhere!"

I felt ashamed and confused and, more than once, crazy. I knew that I had the disease of codependence, and the problem was that I got "rewarded" for it. I was as addicted to people-pleasing as Sandra had been to alcohol, but no one was going to applaud my giving up my addiction; in fact, I would encounter criticism and rejection when I changed my behavior to health instead of enabling.

Other people were my gods, and taking care of them, organizing my life around them, and working hard for their approval was my drug of choice, a drug that distracted me from my lifelong fear of rejection and abandonment. If I could find someone to "help," I would not have to face my own inner fears.

It was in the mid-eighties when I first heard the term "codependence." Listening to Claudia Black speak about the illness of codependence, I felt as if my heart would stop beating. As she described what it was like to grow up in an alcoholic household and what behaviors that kind of environment produced, I had an epiphany.

In my family of origin, there was never any alcohol. There was, instead, an untoward dependence on "church" and "religion," a dependence that had shaped and formed, sometimes deforming, my life and turned me into the people-pleaser I was. My father was a minister, and so it was that the church and its members, its schedule and its financial state, governed our family and we were organized around the needs of the church.

Whatever was going on within the church determined the mood around the dinner table, and I learned early that if I didn't behave myself, my father's job was in jeopardy. That was not paranoia, by the way; it was, in the era of my childhood and adolescence, reality.

The differences in my family and an alcoholic family are significant, but one thing stands out to me. It is easy to recognize and hate the effects of an alcoholic parent and the alcohol itself. It is another issue to hate the way "serving the Lord" takes your parents away from you and keeps you feeling anxious and afraid. It is one thing to hate "the demon rum," but it is guilt-producing to resent the work of God. I learned early to fear others' criticisms, demands, and agendas far more than I feared God.

I am fascinated by the fact that Job's children had parties and that, after those parties, Job offered sacrifices on their behalf, and it makes me know that at the beginning of the book, Job's righteousness was based on external rites and rituals, processes that he looked to for salvation.

I am just as convinced that his personal, searching, moral inventory on the ash heap was leading him to an encounter with the inadequate nature of external processes and the necessity to face one's own false gods and idols in favor of a direct encounter with the Living God who dwells within.

As a child growing up in Sunday school I was taught about what happened to the people in the Bible who clung to the wooden gods they had carved. The children of Israel had been called to worship Yahweh, the One True God, and I thought that idolatry ended with the advent of Jesus.

As a child in a religious tradition that did not allow symbols or statues, I was taught that the various statues that other people had in their churches and homes were meaningless idols, and that it was a sin to worship or pray to those idols. That teaching did not help me to identify the idols that I would choose, idols that would take from me and give nothing back.

As a young person, I had a dim understanding that *some people* had a problem with drugs and alcohol, gambling and sex, but it wasn't until I heard Claudia Black define and describe codependence that I understood that there are other insidious false gods that trap and enslave human beings, sucking from them their life force and their resources, destroying their families, and keeping them from living the abundant life offered by Christ.

What I did not know as a child was that people make idols out of the best parts of life, putting the good gifts of life "on the throne of their lives," as Sandra pointed out in me.

The truth is that people can make an idol out of anything, and whatever has the capacity and potential for blessing and enriching our lives can, taken to the extreme, turn back to bite us. Neither technology, the military or medicine, political power or knowledge can, ultimately, save us, and yet many have put their ultimate faith and trust in those powers external to them.

There is no position, no power or prestige, no pleasure or privilege, and certainly no person who can bear the burden of being "god" to us, and yet we human beings continue to try to make gods in our own image, demanding that those gods give us what they cannot give us, and that is meaning and purpose, love and belonging, salvation. The more we demand that that which we have made with our own hands save us, the greater our unease and disharmony.

There are, as well, those sacred and precious parts of our lives that we serve and enjoy that, unconsciously, we turn into idols. What makes those idolatries so dangerous is that the objects are such good things, and yet marriage and family can become idols, becoming more important than God, and in today's world of hyperparenting, the worship of children is one of the most glaring idols of all.

Job's friends danced around the edges of worshiping the past and making an idol of their own religious system. Sometimes we make an idol of doctrine or a particular ritual, a denomination or an institution, clinging to it as if that thing we have created or inherited can save us. Some make the Bible an idol, and some make one particular concept of God the demigod before whom they bow.

Church, religion, and religious experiences can become the idols of good people, stripping them of their autonomy and free will and turning them into persons who are cut off from their own personal relationship with God because the things of religion or the religious institutions push their way into the foreground.

Patriotism or nationalism can become an idol, so that people get confused and think that God is country and country is god.

Another person can become an idol, and persons can become addicted to caretaking so that they do not feel alive unless they are focused on others.

*

"I know what other people need," I had to confess, "and people like it that I take the initiative to meet their needs. The problem is that I no longer know what I am feeling or needing. I have no idea what I want any more, but I can tell you what others want."

What's wrong with that?

Isn't the rule JOY—"Jesus first. Others second. You last"?

I grew up on that little bromide, and what I learned from that was to ignore my own needs, and over time, that discounting of my own needs led to a slow kind of emotional suicide, which finally showed up as physical symptoms. Indeed, that which is ignored long enough suddenly rises from the depths of the unconscious, demanding attention through a physical symptom, an addictive behavior, or a relationship problem. That which we do not honor in ourselves will be heard one way or another. The very things of which we are unconscious will show up one way or another.

"In today's families, every member's needs must be acknowledged and met," says Dr. James Hollis. "Every member of the family must be nourished and fed in order for the family to be healthy."

In a dysfunctional family, and all families are dysfunctional in some ways and in varying degrees, the family is organized around the most dysfunctional or damaged person, and it is that person who requires the majority of the energy of the family. In that kind of imbalance, some members go without the nourishment they need. In other words, the more dysfunctional the family, the more some members commit emotional or spiritual homicide or suicide.

*

I am curious about what it was about Job that made him think that offering sacrifices on behalf of his children was his responsibility? Was he the one who took over-responsibility in the face of the under-responsibility or outright indifference of his children? Did he, even "way back then," carry the codependent belief that what he did for good could "help" his children or, at the very least, build a hedge high enough that trouble would not reach them? Was he, perhaps, an enabler?

Were Job's actions made out of concern for his children or, unconsciously, out of a self-concern? Was he trying to avoid trouble by intervening on their behalf, and does that ever really work, ultimately?

On the ash heap, Job surely examined himself, and gradually, as he dialogued with his friends, he came to know that whatever was "out there," external to himself, was not the ultimate answer and was not God.

Job discovered that all that he had acquired, achieved, and accomplished, all that had given meaning and purpose to his life, could be snatched away from him in an instant.

Job discovered that all that he had valued and built was destructible and finite. What it took a lifetime to build could vanish in an instant.

Job found that those false gods, as good as they were, were not God and that they weren't nearly big enough for him.

*

I am not saying that God allowed what was most valuable to Job to be snatched from him to punish him. What I am saying is that when we are thrown to the ash heaps, or when we choose to go there to work out our salvation, one of the things we must face is how we have looked to external sources for what only God can give.

I am also saying that, over and over, false gods will either destroy us or we will damage or destroy them. Putting anything other than God as the organizing principle in your life will, ultimately, come back to bite you, showing up in the various symptoms that scream, "There's something wrong here!"

"Seek first the kingdom of God," Jesus said, "and all these things will be added to you."

We must get our priorities straight. We must give our first worship to God, and then, once that is established, our love for all of the other good things in our lives will fall into its proper place.

As I write this chapter, an e-mail comes in, and I pause to read it:

> Grieving several losses/changes of people, places, and things. My role as a mother . . . me being left at home alone. Ex-boyfriend happy in another relationship (ouch, that's an old, very deep wound), job not working out, friendship with the person I've worked with has changed. [I'm] scared and insecure of what my life is going to be . . . taking a long, deep look inside and journaling about the messages/old tapes I've been giving myself about all the above . . . God, this hurts. Wish there was another way to serenity— but I know there's not. I am grateful I've been down this rocky road enough times to know the other side is greater and longer-lasting than the pain I'm in now. I'm feeling cold, small and afraid of my inadequacies, but not of God. My prayer is—May my pain mean something more than how it feels.

Sounds like an encounter with the demigods on the ash heap to me.

*

Dr. James Hollis talks about the "summons" to a larger life that is implicit within our symptoms and our personal pain. "Most of us live in lives too small for our souls," he says, over and over, but never too much, "like Chinese women with their feet bound."

God has flung himself across my path to wake me up to the largeness of life and the ways I am still bound in a life too small, enslaved to one of the false gods who demands service but gives nothing back.

Job, too, was faced with the jealous God who would not allow his servant to remain in an immature state of spiritual grace, slavishly offering sacrifices and jumping higher and harder to meet external standards.

The ornery God flung himself across Job's path, for sure, smashing Job's idols, and he is still in the business of smashing anything we enlightened human beings attempt to turn into a god.

To his friends, Job might be appearing to be in danger of becoming godless, but within the deepest recesses of Job's heart, God was emerging with increased strength and clarity.

Job's friends may have thought he was not telling the truth, but Job was, in fact, coming closer and closer to Truth, closer than his friends had ever imagined. On the ash heap, Job's illusions, lies, deceptions, denials, fantasies, and delusions about God were being burned away.

The friends may have thought that Job was bargaining with God, but Job was learning that we humans do not get to do that.

Job may have come to believe that God was not particularly interested in his comfort, safety, and security, his pleasure or his happiness, but he was also coming to believe that God was deeply interested in his wholeness and in his authenticity.

Job was confident that he would be vindicated. He told the friends that he would be vindicated, and they thought he was arrogant.

I believe that Job's growing confidence was not in his own innocence, but in the presence of God that was beginning to burn within his own heart.

One by one, you have challenged
  my gods.

I've set them up
for myself, each of them,
  thinking they were one thing
when, in fact,

each one has been an idol.
And I thought I could handle them.
I thought I could keep them in their place, but,
   man, are those idols hungry!
I've looked to each one to give me
security and safety,
meaning and purpose,
belonging and pleasure,
     soothing and comfort.
   Each god I've served
 has cost me.

Each one has
exacted a price
from my soul.

   And each one has kept me
from knowing you.

I've pushed this idolatry as far as I can.
I've achieved, accomplished, and acquired.
I've arrived at
the place I've been
traveling to . . .

   One True God.
   Not one of those gods—not one!—
can fill this
hole in my soul.

   God. Yahweh. Truth.
   Each one left me, finally,
empty.
   I found out the hard way.
   Forgive me.
Set me free. Take me back. Grant me your mercy.

Chapter Ten

False Guilt and Cheap Suffering

If you carry guilt two minutes after you have made confession, you are confessing to the wrong god.
—THOMAS KEATING

Sin will either be forgiven . . . or punished. You will either accept the forgiveness of God, or you will find a way to punish yourself. You might as well accept the forgiveness.
—JEANIE MILEY

As I write, a photograph of a butterfly chained to a stake in the ground sits in front of me, a reminder of countless group discussions the picture has stimulated.

"Is the butterfly really chained?" I ask when using the photograph to initiate conversations about the things that keep us chained and bound.

"Or is it lifting the chain?" someone else always asks.

"I think it is a computer-generated photograph!" exclaims a skeptic, thereby ending the discussion until someone suggests that our "stuff" and our "baggage" and, most especially, those things of which we are unconscious always change the way we see anything, just as the computer can change the way we see a butterfly, a chain, and a stake in the ground.

False guilt is like a chain on a butterfly. False guilt prevents you from dealing with true guilt, and it keeps you from flying free. It is hard to lift and heavy to carry. It is sometimes difficult to differentiate from true guilt or shame, and it is, for sure, an illusion. False guilt is often a diversionary tactic, keeping you from looking at the real problem.

The saddest part of all is that false guilt does at least as much damage as true guilt. False guilt is the result of a gross misunderstanding of what sin is, and often it is formed out of the expectations of family and culture and whether or not you live up to those expectations.

*

From the beginning of the book of Job, the author made it clear that no matter what happened to him, Job *did not sin*, and if you work with the definition that sin is separation from God, indeed he did not. In fact, in his extended wrestling match with God, it seems to me that he drew closer and nearer to God with each conversation he had with his friends who so wanted him to make a confession of sin according to their definition.

Job is heroic in standing firm in the face of his friends' silent and spoken demands that he confess sin that he did not commit, insisting that he had done nothing to bring on the tragedies that had turned his life upside down.

It is a tribute to Job's inner strength and centeredness in God that he was able to endure the accusations and implications of his friends and not buckle under them, just to make them feel better or, perhaps, to make a deal with God. Job refused the cheap and easy ways that might get him off the ash heap sooner. He refused to be a liar, just to please his friends. Surely, in his weakness and pain, it would have been easier just to say, "Oh, you must be right. There must be something I'm forgetting, some long-hidden sin that is so far out of my consciousness that I cannot even bring it to mind!"

Instead, something in him—was it God?—gave him the inner strength to trust his own heart and mind. Even if he had made mistakes or human errors, he had not "sinned."

When Job has had enough of his friends' rants and speaks up to them, he is daring to stand up for himself and his innocence, a position that infuriates and insults, confounds and confuses the friends: "I have heard many things like these," he says to them. "Miserable comforters are you all. Will your long-winded speeches never end? What ails you that you keep on arguing? I also could speak like you if you were in my place. I could make fine speeches against you and shake my head at you."

Job did not let his friends hang their own projections on him. He didn't let them turn him into a scapegoat. He didn't succumb to the easy way out of his suffering by going along with what other people thought was wrong with him. Instead, he stood up for himself and waited out his process.

*

What is it about projections and false guilt that keep us bound, chained to others' unconscious material and our own tendency to block the grace and mercy of God?

In the ancient town square in Antwerp, Belgium, on the corner of one of the buildings is a statue of a pregnant woman. The woman, great with child, points to the statue on the corner of the building to her left. That statue, the statue of a man, is pointing to a statue on the corner of the building to his left, and that man is pointing to a third statue on the next building. That last man is, alas, pointing to the pregnant woman.

No one wants to take responsibility or blame for what must be an "unfortunate" pregnancy, and a public one at that. Everyone wants to roll the responsibility off himself and onto someone else. And it is most likely the child who will pay the most dues.

"The kindest thing you can do for the people you love and the culture at large," says Dr. James Hollis, "is to take care of the toxic waste in your own life so that you aren't projecting it out onto someone else."

When I think of projection, the common human practice of seeing in others what we don't see in ourselves and criticizing in others what we cannot face in our own lives, I generally think only about what I am projecting onto others.

However, there is another side to projection, and that is the problem of allowing other people to hang their own unconscious motivations, feelings, and expectations on you! Job's friends, confused and disoriented by his suffering, projected their own inner baggage and their limited understanding of God onto his situation.

Facing your own sin and dealing with it is one of the most crucial and important antidotes to the terrible cultural problem of scapegoating and projection, both of which foster abuse and violence in the home and in the world.

In today's culture, choosing a particular person or a group to hate or fear, making another the enemy or the scapegoat, putting them down so that we can put ourselves up, is a common practice. We seem to need an enemy, someone or something to blame for why things are the way they are, forgetting that it is children who blame, while adults assume responsibility.

In personal relationships, we often project our own needs onto someone, expecting them to do for us what we cannot do for ourselves. We may project our "shadow material," those things we don't want to know about ourselves, onto others, and sometimes we even project the strengths and gifts that we have not identified or don't want to take responsibility for onto someone else, trying to make another person into a hero or a demigod.

Job's friends seemed to want him to admit his guilt so that their own positions and viewpoints could be justified and so that they would feel better. In a way, they wanted Job to be the victim so that their religious system would be vindicated, and if he had done that, he would have avoided the transformational process that was going on at some deep, inner, unseen place in his soul.

*

As I falter and flail, trying to recover from a lifetime of people-pleasing, I so admire Job for not letting his friends back him into the corner of their need to have him conform to their ideas about what was wrong with him. I love Job for refusing their diagnoses, but waiting for God to reveal his truth about his plight, and I am convinced that it is the spirit of God working deep within Job, giving him the strength to wait out God's process.

My preferred method of teaching is dialogical, and as I guide discussions, listening to the input of the members of my classes, I learn along with the class. One day, as the women in my Thursday morning Bible study and I explored the biblical foundations for the Twelve Steps, some of the issues around guilt and shame, it suddenly became clear to me that many of us who were gathered in that room were carrying the burdens of guilt and shame that, in actuality, belonged to someone else.

The women who were in the group were working very hard to come to terms with their own issues. They were taking seriously the challenge of the searching, fearless moral inventory of their lives, often dealing with problems caused by someone else in their personal histories or everyday lives.

Suddenly, I realized that many of us, in taking over-responsibility within a relationship or our families, carry guilt that belongs to someone else, someone who takes under-responsibility!

Sometimes, a loved one is abusive or destructive in any number of ways, but one person will assume responsibility for making things right.

Often, when a husband has an affair, he will come home and begin attacking, criticizing, or blaming his wife, obviously trying to manage his own guilt. And just as often, the wife will go to work, trying to make herself over, working harder and harder to please him, for after all, if she had been more attractive, more patient, more *anything*, he would not have strayed in the first place.

A child gets in trouble in school and starts a fight with a classmate, getting the focus off her and onto the classmate.

A woman, caught in a public scandal, attempts to make her employees take the hit for what she has done.

A secretary, having failed to follow through on a request for a client, tries to cover herself by blaming the client.

If you come from a family whose skeletons are shame-producing, you may be the carrier of that shame, or if there is a family secret, you may have carried the guilt about it for so long that it feels natural. Whatever the cause, it may or may not have had something to do with you, and yet you have chosen to carry the burden of the secret or the guilt, or you, somehow, in your family, got selected to carry it.

When a person is born at the wrong time to parents who couldn't care for them or born the wrong gender, she often carries inherited shame about who she is, living with the disabling messages, "Don't be" or "Don't be you."

False guilt or shame become almost like a curse, trapping the person in behaviors or lifestyles that are just as confining as the chain is to the butterfly in my photograph.

Some of us, I have discovered, were good at being the victim or the scapegoat in our families, for any number of reasons. None of us had voluntarily taken on those roles, waking up one day and deciding, "I think I'll be the scapegoat in my family!" Instead, we had generally drifted into those roles unconsciously, often as children.

Some had taken on the guilt of being a particular race or a particular religion. Growing up poor or wealthy, being slow to learn or gifted, being too successful or a failure, being too strong or too sickly, being the unwanted child or the surviving member of a group or a couple can all create feelings of false guilt, and out of that false guilt or shame, decisions are made that affect the life of the person who carries the guilt and those around her.

Some people live under the false guilt of never being able to do enough or be enough to be at ease in the world. Some carry guilt for being smarter, richer, more popular and successful or healthy than a sibling, a spouse, or a parent.

Whatever the source of the false guilt, it will produce behaviors that "prove" that the guilt is justified, and other people will become accustomed to letting the scapegoat carry the guilt. At some point, however, each of us is invited into the liberating processes of differentiating between what is true guilt and what is false, what belongs to you and what is not yours to carry.

That which we do not know about ourselves, and the things we know but refuse to deal with in a healthy way, will eventually show up in a symptom or a problem. Often, what one generation refuses to face will be carried by the next generation so that the parents' dues are exacted from the children, and always with a high interest rate.

If I were running the schools of the world, I would teach all children the skills of forgiveness. I would teach them how to own their own stuff and take responsibility for it, and I would make sure that they didn't leave school until they knew how to make amends to the people they have hurt.

And if I were running the churches of the world, I would make sure that the confessional booth was reinstated. Perhaps the practice would not be required of people, and I might want to make it be a little more like the restoration steps of Alcoholics Anonymous, but I would make it possible for people to have healthy ways to confess their sins within the community of faith. That is, I think, at least as important as church athletic teams and genealogy groups.

*

Sin, as I understand it, is not the same thing as a mistake or a human error. It is not so much the faults and failures that we carry because we are fallible human beings, but it is separation from God or, to go along with the archery term, "missing the mark."

Most of us confess behaviors and symptoms as our sins. All of us wear masks and assume roles that hide who we really are, what we really are thinking, and what we really do want and feel, but underneath what is often called "the false self," the "big sins" are actually the afflictive feelings that fuel and feed the self-defeating and harmful behaviors. Indeed, those afflictive feeling grow out of that basic separation from God and from the true self that we are.

The big sins are hate and anger, shame and guilt, feelings of inferiority and inadequacy, and fear. All our troubling behaviors can be tracked back, according to this model, to one of these four "demons," or sins.

According to Job's friends, his problem was guilt. He had, obviously, done something to bring about his terrible suffering, and so, in their simplistic way of thinking, if he would just get on about the business of identifying his sin and guilt, he could be forgiven and get on about his life. And they could get on with theirs.

It is popular in today's culture to discount guilt as a useless emotion, but, in truth, it is healthy and appropriate for a person to feel guilt for the things he has done that have hurt himself or another person. When you have done something, either intentionally or out of unconsciousness or ignorance, that has harmed another, it is a sign of maturity to own up to it, to confess it, and, wherever you can, to make amends and to seek to do whatever you can to make repairs.

False guilt, however, is the guilt that continues long after you have made confession. It is the guilt that continues to plague you, even after you have made your confession and attempted to make amends. It is that terrible feeling that you are, somehow, wrong and bad. Unfortunately, many religious systems thrive on keeping people feeling wrong and bad and, therefore, in need of the system for redemption.

Of the many problems that false guilt produces is cheap suffering, and it is cheap because it is not authentic suffering. Cheap suffering is cheap because it is suffering about the wrong problem in order to avoid the real problem.

Cheap suffering is cheap because it is more about moaning and groaning and singing the blues than it is authentic lament and remorse, which lead to authentic confession. It is cheap because it never goes anywhere good, but pulls you downward in a cycle of self-abuse, self-flagellation, and self-pity.

Cheap suffering is cheap because it makes people take on the burdens that, in reality, belong to someone else, thereby depriving the person carrying that burden from facing his own stuff (It's easier to carry your problem than mine!), and it prevents the person whose problem it really is from having to grow up and face himself (I like it when you do my work for me; then I don't have to!).

Cheap suffering is self-flagellation. It is beating up on myself just because it is a habit, perhaps copying behavior imported from childhood. Cheap suffering is running myself down, criticizing myself, intimidating myself, and holding myself in someone else's chains. It is not living up to the freedom we have been granted. It is labor pains without any result. It is whining and calling that suffering.

In my lifetime, I have learned that it is my job to assume 100 percent responsibility for what is my part in any conflict or problem in my life, and I have learned that that really is all I can handle. Taking on what does not belong to me is a way to avoid my own responsibility, my own real guilt, and is, therefore, cheap suffering. It always leads me around in circles in a pattern where the real issues don't get solved, the actual problems never are resolved, and the same, habitual, repetitive, life-sucking behaviors go on and on.

*

The earliest Ash Wednesday service at Palmer Memorial Episcopal Church is a quiet, simple, and contemplative service. There aren't many of us who attend this service, and that is one of the reasons I love it. At the evening service, the church is packed with people, and all the stops are pulled out with music, liturgy, and incense. I love that service as well.

Palmer Church is the church where my granddaughter, Madeleine, was baptized, but it's been my "Ash Wednesday" church for some time. Situated among tall oak trees that line Main Street in Houston, Palmer is right between the campus of Rice University and the Texas Medical Center. It is, for many reasons, an unusually sacred space for me.

While my own tradition does not include the observance of Ash Wednesday, in general, there was in me something that began to long to take the days leading up to Easter more seriously. I began to long for the act of kneeling, and then, having experienced the health-giving grace of confession, I wanted to make confession and the receiving of forgiveness, spoken by another human being, a part of my regular spiritual practice.

There came a day when it was not enough for me just to sit in the pew and pass the plate of the Communion bread and the cup. I needed to get up off my laurels and walk to the front to receive the elements as a physical expression of my willingness to do my part to meet God.

This year, as I slipped into the quiet space of Palmer Church, I found my favorite pew, pulled the kneeling bench down, and knelt to pray. City noises, muffled by the stone walls, nevertheless reminded me of the busy, hurried world outside, a world I love and find filled with delight.

Please, please remove anything in me that is bigger than you are! a voice within me almost screamed as soon as my knees hit the kneeling bench. Later, I realized that in my prayer was an invitation to face my own false gods, for anything bigger in my mind and in my life than God is an idol.

Please remove from my mind and heart any of the burdens that don't belong to me, burdens I am carrying that belong to someone else.

Sitting back in the pew, I took a deep breath, deeper than in a long time, and listened to the words that had I just spoken from some deep place within my heart. I knew that part of my Lenten journey was going to be giving up the burdens that don't belong to me. I knew that I was being called to give up my false guilt and confess what was true guilt. Other people's *stuff* had become too big in my inner world, and it was time for the things that were blocking me to be released so that God could take center stage in my consciousness.

Taking over-responsibility for others' choices and lives, "trespassing" in others' processes, and taking on what did not belong to me had filled my mind with worries and concerns. I needed to take my own life back.

"Forgive me my trespasses," I whispered silently, "and forgive those who have trespassed against me."

Boundaries! Boundaries! Learning and finessing the delicate issues of boundaries takes me off the ash heap of false guilt and sets me on solid and safe ground.

Waiting for the service to begin, I thought of Job, waiting on his ash heap, and I took courage in that hero who endured his own suffering, but refused the seduction of cheap suffering for what did not belong to him.

I have learned that when you can take full responsibility of what belongs to you, but only what belongs to you, then you are making steps toward freedom.

O Lord—
I've heard that you are merciful.

**I've heard that you draw near
to the broken-hearted and that
you are full of grace.**

> **You've also been known to turn
> a woman into a block of salt,
> and you've been known to confound the wise.**

**And so it is with a little
bit of fear and trepidation—
and a big lot of yearning—
that I come to you
and ask that you
sift and sort it all out for me.**

Show me, please, the truth
about my sin.
Give me clarity about what
you don't like and what it is
that others don't like—that may not,
after all, bother you at all!

That pure heart I've heard about?
That's what I want!

Create in me—oh, God, please
create in me—
a clean heart so that
I don't get mixed up about what
it is I should confess

and what it is I can release into
your mercy.
I want to mourn for what is real,
but I don't want to
weep and wail for what is false.

Please speak louder than my lesser gods.
Please quiet my idols and their incessant voices.

Please, in the deepest chambers of my heart,
plant your Truth . . . your Way . . . your Light.

Why Be Good. . .If Nobody's Watching?

If you've come here to hear me confess my sins,
I'll tell you that I wish I had sinned more.
—A DYING MAN TO HIS PRIEST

Be good . . . and you'll be lonely.
—MARK TWAIN

I want to be liked! I want to be popular instead of respected!
—A TEARFUL SEVENTH-GRADER

When I was a child, each Sunday my father gave me my offering to take to church and a small envelope printed with a place for my name and several squares for checking certain behaviors and adding up, at the end, the points earned by that behavior. Attending and being on time counted, as did bringing my Bible, studying the Sunday school lesson, making contacts during the week, bringing a visitor, and staying for worship.

Faithfully, I put my offering in the envelope, licked it, and then checked all the squares. I always made a 100.

I am not proud to admit that it was more important to me, as the preacher's daughter, to check all of those squares than it was to tell the truth.

Looking good and looking as if I had done all the right things was actually an act of self-preservation, for my mother had told me that if I did not behave myself, my daddy would have to resign. Sadly, in the religious culture of my childhood, that was a true statement, so, from childhood, I carried the heavy burden of making and keeping the "right" appearances in order to protect my father's job.

Often, as an adolescent, I refrained from particular activities not because I was so holy and pure, but because I was more afraid of the censure of church members. Believe me, in that era, such belief was not paranoia; it was self-preservation.

What that behavior taught me was duplicity, and it made me become inordinately concerned with meeting external standards, placating authority figures, and gaining others' approval. I really was a "good little girl," but I was good at least some of the time out of fear.

On the other hand, I wanted to follow the rules and made my parents proud, not only in front of the church members. I've often wondered, however, if my goodness was more about staying out of trouble and out of the line of criticism than it was real goodness. My "goodness" was not so much the goodness of conscious, mature, and responsible choosing as it was goodness out of the fear of consequences if I were "bad," whatever "bad" might mean.

*

The very first thing we learn about Job is that he was a righteous man and that even after the things he valued most were stripped from him, he "did not sin." On the ash heap, then, surely he had to reassess what it meant to be good and righteous. In the face of his friends' accusations that he had done something bad, Job must have done some serious thinking about what makes a person good.

It seems to me that, in meeting the external requirements of "a good man," "a good family man," "a good religious leader," Job had worked really hard. Was he, however, working from the inside out or the outside in? Was his goodness about looking good or about being good at his core?

Jesus had harsh words for the keepers of the law who were all polished up on the outside, but filthy on the inside. Jesus wasn't into appearance and image, and he called people who were "whitewashed tombs."

The false self, or ego, of Job was put on trial, and it was a severe trial. The trial, however, was setting free the innate and authentic goodness of Job.

*

Is it "goodness" if it has never been tested in the white-hot fire of temptation? What is goodness, anyway? Is it about behavior, or is it about a person's character? Can you do good things out of selfish or evil motivations, and are those things still "good"?

Confronted by his wife's despair and her admonition to "curse God and die!" did Job examine his attitudes and behavior, searching for what was left in his life that was good? Did he wonder if, given a chance, he could be good again?

What does it mean, after all, to be good? Is being good a good thing? Why do some people try so hard to be good, and others, seemingly, try so hard to be bad?

Is it goodness if you have to try? Or is it goodness only if it flows naturally from the way you are?

Why do people want their children to "be good"? Is it for the children's sake or to make the parents look like good parents?

Is it goodness if you're just trying to stay out of trouble?

Is it goodness if your main concern is avoiding pain and suffering?

It is goodness when it is simple self-concern, self-preservation, or, perhaps, good common sense?

Is it goodness if what you really want are rewards, medals, and honors?

Is it goodness if you are trying to get people to like you by your good behavior?

Are you being good if you behave in such a way to earn respect and avoid criticism?

Is it goodness if your goal is to get people to trust you, to follow you, to buy from you, or to hire you?

Does being good count if what you are really trying to do is get people to do things for you or take care of you?

Is it being good if your actions are intended to help you fit in and belong?

Is goodness simply the absence of badness?

*

"Why do you keep on doing that?" I was asked about an irritating behavior, and I stuttered and stammered my weak response. "I'm just trying to be . . . nice," was all I could say.

"Yeah, and how's that working for you?" was the quick and impudent question coming back to me.

Sitting on my own ash heap, I came to the point when I had to admit, finally, that being nice and being good were going to have to be redefined. I had to acknowledge that being nice and being good were adaptive responses I had developed when I was a very young child, responses that I made to life situations in order to stay safe and to avoid rejection or criticism.

Are Mr. Nice Guy, the People-Pleaser, and the Goody-Two-Shoes really good, or are they simply compliant, adaptive, and self-concerned?

And is it true that any virtue, carried too far, can become a vice? It is possible that what is perceived as goodness in one culture or era or family might, in another time and place, do harm?

In my life, I have discovered that when I carry being nice too far, as an accommodation to someone else or to an authority figure outside myself, I usually wind up hurting myself, violating my own integrity, or sacrificing my own autonomy. And when someone else goes along with what I want just to be nice, but hates doing it, there's always a kickback.

There is a very fine, thin, but real, line between being nice and accommodating, and being dishonest and manipulative.

Most of the time, when you ask people to define goodness, the definitions are about what people don't do instead of what they do, and often the definitions are more about what people do instead of who they are.

Often, people will turn to the Ten Commandments as a standard of measurement for goodness, but what you get when you push that too far is what Jesus confronted in the legalism of his day.

When I was a child and adolescent, I operated with a narrow view of what it meant to be good, and mostly it was about pleasing my parents. Somehow, when I was an adolescent, my understanding of the biblical heroes made those men and women into sanitized saints.

In adulthood, however, my understanding has been turned inside out with a more comprehensive reading of the stories of Jacob and his several women; David, "the man after God's own heart," and Bathsheba; Rahab, the prostitute; and Tamar, the seductress. The story of Ruth's being instructed by her mother-in-law to go and lie down with Boaz would not have fit into my childhood or adolescent definition of goodness.

For people who cry out for us to return to "biblical family values," I have to ask, "Just which one of the families do you want to emulate?"

*

I believe that whatever human "goodness" is, it has to be about our reflecting the image of God, and certainly we can all agree that *God is good.*

What is the goodness of God, however, for the person who has just lost everything that means anything to him?

Is God good to the person whose health or loved one has been snatched from her?

What about the wrath of God? Is that . . . *goodness?*

Is it goodness when it feels so bad that you think you cannot bear it?

The goodness of God has to flow from the reality that God's nature is love and that God's love is active, dynamic, life-giving, and re-creative. The goodness of God embraces all of the facets of God's character that we see revealed in the Scriptures, and our human goodness is a reflection of that nature of God.

Perhaps the goodness of God is the life force of God, coursing throughout all of creation.

Perhaps the goodness of God is mercy, grace, and love, extended toward us, alive in us, surrounding us and animating all of creation.

Perhaps goodness is not so much about purity and what we don't do as it is accepting that we, as the creatures, are invited into a participation and partnership with God, fully engaged in life as we access and appropriate the abundant life that Jesus came to show us and give us.

*

Sitting at a stop sign on one of the busiest streets of Houston, I marveled at the flowers that bloom year round in my adopted city. I was on my way to teach the book of Job at St. Luke's United Methodist Church with serious seekers I have come to love over the years. They had sat strong with me during the days my husband was in the hospital, giving me encouragement as I worried and fretted and cared for him.

I had spent the afternoon wrestling through some tough issues with some of my spiritual directees, and in between, I had talked with one of my daughters about a rough patch in her own life. After the class, I would go home and rock my oldest granddaughter or my grandson who lived with us, with their mother, for a few months.

I was bone tired, frightened and discouraged, feeling overwhelmed with what life had handed me, just about the time I thought I could prop up my feet and coast on into my "mastery" years. I was committed, however, to living the faith I was teaching and, to the best of my ability, to walking my talk.

"How are you?" people would ask during those dark days when my husband was so ill.

"Around the edges, I'm exhausted and I'm frightened," I would say, "but at my core, I'm calm and tranquil."

There at the stoplight, I recalled Jesus' declaration that he had come to bring abundant life, a Scripture from the book of John that had set me on a quest to know and understand the life and teachings of Jesus, and I had to smile.

For years, I had had such a narrow view of what I thought abundant life really was, confining that abundance to what I defined as the good things, the blessings, the gifts and fruit of the spirit of God. In the late fall afternoon, however, I suddenly realized that when you sign on for the abundant life, you are committing to full-engagement living so that you get it all.

Abundant life is infinitely more than "the good life" as defined by contemporary culture. In the deepest and richest sense the abundant life is the fullness of life. It is bounty and it is extravagance, all coming from different directions, and all of it with a lesson or a challenge, a burden or a blessing, a crisis or an opportunity, sadness and joy.

Life is not good or bad, but a mixture of all kinds of experiences. It is not black or white, and only for the unimaginative is it gray. Instead, life is a vibrant plaid with dark hues and light ones, and among the various colors, there is often a thread of gold.

The abundant life is not about external things. The "good life" isn't about what you can achieve, accomplish, or acquire. The good life is not about performance or productivity, position, prominence, or privilege.

The abundant life is life lived with a sense of the Divine Presence who is in you, around you, above you, and beneath you, giving you life in the way you need it.

God cannot be other than God is, and it seems to me that a "good person" is a person who lives from the core of his own unique and true self, conforming his outer behavior to the directives from within instead of living to please or placate the external world.

A good person behaves in ways that are consistent with who she is instead of trying to fit some role or expectation of who others think she should be, and that is called authenticity.

A good person cooperates and collaborates with God in doing things that benefit others and stopping things that hurt others.

And a good person never forgets what it means to be human.

*

As children of God, we are made in the very image of God, created just a little lower than angels. And . . . we are sinners. On top of all of that, we who call ourselves Christian are brothers and sisters in Christ. It's a lot to ask of frail human beings, yet the Scriptures include all three realities.

Driving home from a recent church retreat at Laity Lodge, I had plenty of time to think about our speaker's wisdom and what it means to carry the responsibility and burden of the multifaceted dimensions of being human. Pondering the trouble we humans have getting along in the family of God as brothers and sisters in Christ, it occurred to me that perhaps that is partly because we forget that each of us and all of us carry *both* the image of God and the tendency to sin.

It is an immature mind and childish thinking that insists that life fall into either/or, black/white, good/bad categories, being one or the other and not allowing for both. More than one thing can be true about almost everything and anyone, at any given moment, and maturity requires that our brains flex and bend enough to wrap around two realities at the same time. It is a grown-up who can manage to tolerate ambiguity and ambivalence, paradox and irony, and not lose his mind in the process!

It makes an enormous difference how I live in my community of faith when I can hold all three parts of my identity in tension, and I am a healthier member of the body of Christ and a more loving and compassionate sister in Christ when I remember that my identity encompasses behavior, attitudes, and speech that reflect an accurate image of myself.

I am, in fact, loving and non-loving. I can be generous and stingy. I am capable of being forgiving, tolerant, and compassionate, as well as vindictive, intolerant, and punitive. I have within me the capacity for tenderness and patience, and sometimes within the same day, I shock myself with my self-centeredness and insensitivity, toughness and my impatience.

I am courageous and fearful, noble and petty, selfless and selfish, often responding out of forces that I did not know existed in the underworld of my unconsciousness.

On any given day, I can behave as a mature adult and a petulant child, a cranky old woman and an idealistic adolescent!

It makes a big difference when I hold in consciousness the reality that my fellow brothers and sisters in Christ are, as well, made up of the complex and complicated motivations that I am and that all are made in the image of God *and* inclined to fall short of the glory of God.

And so, as we frail and fallible human beings stumble and falter together, attempting to be kingdom people while we strive to pay our bills and raise our children, solve our problems and fulfill our goals, we must be as patient with each other as God is with us.

Some people just want the "made in the image" side of human nature, and others focus only on our sin nature. Surely we are called to the high and holy task of calling forth in each other that image of the Divine that is stamped within our innermost being.

Surely we are called to give up being surprised at the sin nature in each other and use that energy, instead, to forgive one another. Perhaps, if we can remember who we really are, and all of who we are, we can be better siblings in the kingdom of God.

*

The heart of Job was being broken open, and on the ash heap he was being deepened and matured. The goodness of God was doing serious business with Job, bringing forth the essential goodness of his servant.

When my middle daughter, Julie, was about three, I was rubbing her back one night as she was going to sleep. Suddenly, she roused from that liminal state right between wakefulness and slumber and said, "God thinks I'm one of the goodest little girls he ever made!"

Delighted, I grabbed her in my arms and hugged her, assuring her that that was the truth, silently praying that she would always feel that sense of God's pleasure in her.

Later, as she entered adolescence, she began to do what was her job to do and that was push the limits and test the boundaries, all necessary preparation for making the huge leap from home out into the world. She tested my patience constantly, but it was hard to punish her because she made all As, didn't get into any trouble, and was loved by almost everyone, at least everyone we knew!

On weekends, she loved to move from one event to another with her friends, often calling in from one home to announce her plans, and on the first Sunday night of Advent when she was fourteen, she pushed the time limit just as far as she could. Arriving home past the time when we were supposed to leave for the church and the service of the Hanging of the Greens, I was furious with her.

All the way to the church, we argued, and when we arrived at the church, she and her sister got out of the car, slamming the doors, and took off toward the building, leaving me to walk across the darkened parking lot by myself. All the way into the building, I berated myself, telling myself that I was the worst mother in the world, and once inside, the lights and decorations almost seemed to mock me. I did, indeed, need the advent of new life.

The sanctuary was beautiful and filled with people. Alone, I made my way to the front, crowding into a single seat in front of my pediatrician and his wife. My husband, the pastor, was occupied with the pre-service preparations, and I felt lonely in that crowd, even though it was my own community of faith.

At the time in the service when the children, dressed in their Christmas finery, went to the back of the sanctuary to get the poinsettias, I glanced behind me, watching them scampering and dancing with the fun of it all. Suddenly, Julie got up from the very back of the room and began walking toward the center of that back section.

What is she doing now? I asked myself drearily.

I saw her lean down, and when she stood up, she was holding Jana Pearce in one arm and, in the other, a pot of poinsettias. With my heart in my throat and tears coursing down my face, I watched my daughter carry Jana down to the altar. When they got there, Julie knelt down so that Jana could take the pot of poinsettias and place them, alongside the other children's, on the altar.

My pediatrician turned to me and patted my shoulder. With tears in his eyes, he said, "She's going to be O.K.," and I knew that he was right.

Jana Pearce had been born into our community of faith eight years before, stunning all of us because she was born with spina bifida. Our church had embraced her with love and had given her parents support and encouragement, and we had watched Jana become a feisty little girl with lots of spunk. She was, in a way, the darling of the church.

That night, back at home, I knocked on Julie's door, and when she opened the door and let me in, I said, "That was the sweetest thing I have ever seen in church." She tried to shrug it off, as if it were nothing, and so I apologized for the harsh words I had said before church and turned to leave her room.

"Mom," she said to me, and of course I stopped and turned back toward her. "She needed to go to the altar with the other kids, and no one was taking her."

*

Last year, I led a retreat for First Baptist Church of Lewisville, Texas, and Jana Pearce, now a lovely and beautiful young woman, was one of the participants. At lunch, she and her mother, Lana, and I ate together, and Jana told me how her mother takes her every day to college classes.

"What are you studying, Jana?" I asked her, and she quickly described the occupational therapy classes she was taking.

"Don't you know how many people there are out there like me who need somebody to help them?" she asked, and my eyes filled with tears.

"Now, tell me," she continued, spunky as ever, "where is that Julie?"

That Julie, my daughter, was completing her residency in pediatrics at Baylor College of Medicine in Houston. Every day, she was encountering children who, like Jana, needed someone to take them to the altar of healing and redemption, mercy and grace.

When Julie was being a typical adolescent, she wasn't being bad. She was doing what was natural. When she carried Jana to the altar, she was being so good I could hardly stand it, and when Jana Pearce lives as a symbol of hope and optimism in the face of her own suffering, that is the goodness of God, alive and pulsating in creation.

The goodness of God is mediated day after day through imperfect and broken human beings who are willing to participate with him in extending love and mercy and cups of cold water to others. Goodness is not about being in a state of sinless perfection, whatever that is, but it is about opening your mind and heart enough to get up and meet a human need, loving someone in the name of God, doing what you can with what you have . . . and, sometimes, you carry another person to the altar.

Listen, God—
Programmed early to be good,
I did "good" well, and with every
layer of goodness,
I left a little part of my true self
behind, hidden
underneath
lovely accommodations
and pleasing adaptations.

I did "nice" well, too, even
when I didn't mean it.
In fact, I think I was even
better at "nice" when I didn't mean it.
I could lay "nice" on really thick, slathering
it like rancid
butter and
stopping up the veins of my
own heart with my
very own duplicity and
falseness.

God, this doesn't work for me now.
The masks I have worn are suffocating me.
I can hardly bear my false self,
and surely it is my falseness
that is a stench in your nostrils.

the more I've tried to be the whitest
sheep of all your white sheep, the more I
became the black sheep. The more I've tried not to be
the prodigal child, the more I've
become the sourpuss elder child,
refusing to come to your party.

And yet, somehow, in the coming clean,
I hear not your censure or your shaming, but
a glad yelp, as if you are laughing and slapping
your knee and throwing back your head and
shouting, "Welcome home! This black sheep
of mine
has finally come back home.
Come home to herself.
Come home to my heart, where she
belongs."
I've come home, come home, come home,
come home!

Chapter Twelve

Giving Up

The terror and wonder of the Book of Job is that God slowly allows Job to walk through the stages of grief and dying, while admittedly, holding his feet to the fire.
—RICHARD ROHR

Let go . . . and let God.
—SLOGAN FOR RECOVERING PEOPLE

"I was at the end of my rope last week," my friend Betty Cody said, reporting in to the group of women who have gathered at St. Luke's Methodist Church in Houston all of this year to study Job. "I was so tired. I have dealt with this problem for so long," she continued. As we had studied Job, she had dealt with various health challenges of her husband and then her daughter's cancer.

I have often said that if I am ever in crisis, I would want Betty Cody near me, for she exudes strength, mercy, and compassion, born of a lifetime of tender and informed caregiving. A nurse for fifty years, she has been at the top of her field in nursing education at M. D. Anderson Cancer Center, teaching, writing, and speaking across the country about caring for cancer patients. I have listened in awe to her stories about her work with the prison system through the Episcopal diocese. Betty knows how to be with others in their suffering. She has also spent time on the ash heap of her own suffering.

The women in this group are not casual seekers. They aren't content to skate around the edges of reality, and they aren't willing to accept simple solutions for complex problems. Full of empathy, they have become willing to share each other's burdens, and so they understood what our friend was saying. Most of us in that class have been driven to that end of the rope Betty Cody described.

"I went home and got on my ash heap," our friend told us. "I came to the place of giving up, and it is amazing how different this week has been."

"Getting on the ash heap" sounded to me a great deal like "getting on a nest," and in some ways this feminine image is appropriate, for we can voluntarily go to a place of surrender. We don't always have to be pushed there, but we can consciously go into the silence of the inner sanctuary of the heart and "brood over" our problems and the darkness of the chaos, just as the spirit of God brooded over the void in creating the world.

Later still, my friend confided in me the specifics of how things were "softening" in her life, how she was handling her difficulties in a new way, and how the walls she had not been able to force down were coming down naturally, and she attributed that shift in the problem to her act of surrender.

*

Thomas Keating, the Benedictine monk who has developed and taught the practice of Centering Prayer around the world, describes the work of what he calls "the Divine Therapist" that happens in the practice of Centering Prayer. In the practice, the "prayer word" is chosen as an expression of the person's intention to consent to the presence and action of Christ, who dwells within the inner kingdom. Keating describes the process of the dismantling of the "false self," or the ego, which happens as the inner Self is nurtured and strengthened by the consistent practice of prayer.

To practice the discipline of Centering Prayer is to consent to the mysterious work of the Holy Spirit, or the Divine Therapist, at the deep level of the unconscious mind, where ego, ego defenses, and ego constraints do not have the upper hand. Over time, the work of the Divine Therapist addresses the "emotional programming of a lifetime," as Keating describes it, forming a person's inner life around a new system of belief and of life rather than the limited and limiting beliefs from childhood.

In the story of Job, the friends pounded away on Job's ego, trying to make him confess and conform to what the ego—theirs and his!—would prefer, and that is what all egos prefer: safety and security, predictability and comfort. At the deepest level of Job's life, however, in places that could not be seen or controlled by the ego messages, the Divine Therapist was at work, re-forming Job and bringing forth the true self.

Back and forth the friends and Job go, "dialoguing" about Job's plight, until I have to wonder which was harder for Job to deal with: his losses or the unrelenting accusations and advice from his friends. I am afraid that I would have buckled under the onslaught of verbiage from my friends. I would have cried for relief from their arguments. I would have begged for them to stop and go away, but perhaps it was their persistence that pushed Job to the limits of his endurance. Perhaps they were necessary to bring him through his stages of grief to the point of surrender and acceptance.

It is one thing to be driven to the end of your endurance when you have not bothered with God or have, in fact, openly and consciously defied God. Atheists suffer the terrors and losses of life. Every human being has *issues*.

There is another layer of agony in coming to the place of giving up when you have built your life on the belief that you could count on God in a pinch. To have served God faithfully, only to come to the place of losing everything that was meaningful to you, has its own kind of bitter taste to it.

What was crashing for Job, on the ash heap of his losses, was a religious system based on reward and punishment, and his secret or unconscious bargain with God was in his face and pounding in his ears, coming from his friends and, surely, echoing in his own mind and heart. "Where did I miss the signs?" we often ask, when things blow up in our face. "How could I have been so mistaken?" we wonder when what seemed like a sure deal turns into a disaster.

One of the slogans of recovering people is "Let go . . . and let God," and people who have tried that will talk about how hard it is to let go of a substance, a practice, or a person. It is hard to let go of attitudes, behaviors, and habits that keep you stuck in a self-defeating cycle. It is hard to let go of that which has given you, though temporarily and with destructive outcomes, solace and comfort, soothing and escape.

Job had to let go of the things that had been stripped from him, and sometimes it is easier to let go when you are flat on your back and the fact that you have no choice whatsoever is inescapable. As long as a person has one more trick up his sleeve, one more resource he can mine, one more thing he can do, giving up is often prolonged. Sadder and more destructive, however, are the illusions of grandeur, the delusions of denial, and the fantasies of escape that prevent people from ever coming to the point of giving up.

"I thought I could outrun it," a friend told me about his problems, "but it was too big for me." His life lay in disarray around him. There was no way to recall all of the bad decisions he had made over a lifetime, decisions that seemed, in the moment, innocuous and harmless enough. "It was my pride that got me," he continued, and it was my job to tell him that at the end of our extremity is the place where God is often the most creative, productive, and helpful. It is when we have no other options that God seems to love to work.

*

"The barn's burned down," says the poet. "Now I can see the moon." Without the protective layers to which we have clung, we finally have the possibility of seeing and hearing God, who has been there all along.

Job had no choice but to let go of his attachment to the external things that had given his life meaning and purpose. His other layers of relinquishment were harder, however.

Giving up his dependence upon his old system of currying favor with God would take some time. Letting go of his former ways of seeing himself, God, and the world couldn't happen overnight. Letting go of the old, without anything new out there in front of him, was a huge risk for Job, and so it is with us.

Sometimes, too, you have lived with a particular pain for so long that you don't even know whom you would be if you didn't have it. It may be that all evidence in the present moment indicates that you don't need to hold on to that feeling of inferiority, that fear of not having enough, the pain of a childhood wounding, the failure of your life, and yet you cling to it, almost as a way of punishing yourself over and over again. Letting go of pain and stepping into joy is, strangely, sometimes an impossible task.

"Do you know what would make you happy?" I asked one of my spiritual directees one day, and as I expressed that question, I was aware that I was really asking, "Do you want to be well?"

I've always been fascinated by Jesus' question to the man who had been lying on a mat by the pool of Bethesda, waiting for thirty years to get to the healing waters but always finding someone to blame for his inability to do that.

"What do you mean?" she asked me, puzzled. Each week, her growing dissatisfaction with the way things were in her life was the focus of her sharing with me. I could sense that as long as she was governed by all the things she didn't like and all the things that were wrong in her life, and there were quite a few, there was not room in her mind or attention for the joys of life. However, it seemed to me that her primary and comfortable ego position was one of being unhappy, dissatisfied, and out of sorts.

In listening to people, in the holy space of what is called "spiritual direction," I am acutely aware that it is not up to me to direct the person, telling her what to do with her life, or, God forbid, to attempt to direct God! Instead, I see it as my job, and my privilege, to sense with the directee the direction the spirit of God is taking in the person's life.

Often, the pain and suffering the person expresses is the place where God does want to work, and sometimes all I am called to do is listen and pray for the person, and sometimes I can ask questions or make suggestions. At other times, I sense that the issue is a therapeutic issue, and I can suggest that analysis or therapy may be an appropriate "ash heap" on which to encounter this problem at a deeper level.

Sometimes, however, focusing on the pain is a defense against happiness and a resistance to feeling good, a fear of being healed and of the challenges of "rising and walking." A continued retelling of the same story may be indicative of an addiction to the pain or the unhappiness and an avoidance of taking responsibility for some part of life.

On that particular day, then, I asked this directee to begin looking for the things in her life that were good and to make a list of the things she enjoyed, not as an exercise in avoiding the pain of her life, but as a way of accommodating both ends of the spectrum of life in her awareness. I challenged her to let go of her negativity and fear, and she met the challenge.

The agony of letting go is often in the terror of not being able to see what it is "out there" that will give you security, meaning, and purpose, if anything, and so most of us will fight and resist as long as we can. It is as if the thing you cannot release is a security blanket, a transitional object that gives you a false feeling of safety and comfort. Using another metaphor, when you let go of one trapeze and reach for the one that is swinging to you, there is a terrifying moment when you are caught in the air, between trapezes.

*

"You need to say yes sooner," my friend Keith Hosey told me. "Stop resisting how things are and start allowing them to be just as they are, in the moment."

"I'm doing the best I can," I told him, and then, in the quietness of my prayer time, I knew that I might have been doing the best I could, up to that moment, but I was not yet doing the best I knew.

I had to face the truth that I knew better, though I wasn't doing better at letting go of the small things all during the day. I was holding on to my old patterns in such subtle and unconscious ways, and so, rising to his challenge, I began to become conscious of the ways I was resisting the press of the Spirit in my life.

Recovering people often get stuck and trapped in doing the "two step." Given enough pain, a recovering person can admit he is powerless over a substance, a practice, or a person, and that his life has become unmanageable. Then, it is relatively easy (and harder for some than for others) to take either that Second Step, coming to believe that there is a power greater than himself that can restore him to sanity, or the Twelfth Step, where he tells his story and brings another person into the program. It is the Steps in between where the hard work of recovering happens, and many people do not make it past the challenge of the Third Step and turn their wills and their lives over to the care of God as they understand God.

You can spend your life avoiding letting go, but you take the rewards that go along with that. You can wiggle out of acceptance of what is and abandonment of your life into the hands of God, but in doing that you miss the mighty acts of God's transforming grace and mercy. You don't ever have to deal with your "stuff"; you can spend a lifetime in avoidance and denial, and people do that all the time.

What Job shows us is that, in giving up his will to God, God finally has the opportunity to work in the midst of the sorrow.

*

For Job, coming to that place of giving up was a terrible, laborious, and tedious battle. In his last words, as he is hobbling toward the end of his arguments, he laments the past. He bemoans the way people treat him and the anguish in his own physical body. He shudders under the mocking of the young, and he wails the way God has refused to answer him.

Job reminded God of the things he had done for him and the things he had not done, and then he yearns for someone to come to his defense, to hear him, to plead his case. And then he stops speaking, and it is apparent that he has come to a point of no return.

Job's pattern in dealing with his sorrow is so like ours. We stumble and falter as we grieve, taking two steps forward and three back. We make a little progress in overcoming our anguish, and then we regress, falling backward into the pit once again.

It would be so much easier if our grieving were neat and tidy, as it is lined out in Elisabeth Kübler-Ross's stages that move the bereaved from denial to anger, and then to bargaining and depression until, finally, acceptance is reached. In my experience, persons can stay in denial for a very long time before they cycle over into anger, lashing out at others, sometimes innocent bystanders and often those closest to them. The stage of bargaining can take a long time or a short time, while the person tries to find ways to avoid the hard challenge of letting go of that which was so important.

In the bargaining stage of grief, people often read one more book about their problem, attend one more seminar, seek out one more doctor, or one more treatment plan, a geographic change, a job change, or a new spouse. "This time, it will work," a bargain-hunter will say. "Maybe this is the answer to my problem." In the beginning of the bargaining stage, looking for "the answer" feels, and can actually be, empowering. Stuck in that stage, however, the pursuit of one more thing to ameliorate or eradicate the pain is simply running away from the problem and the pain.

If the process of grieving is to continue, however, the person finally comes to the point of having to admit that all of the best resources in the world are not enough to take away the pain. Coming closer to the moment of acceptance, a person may choose to cycle back to anger. Or he may, out of self-protection, which is not protection at all, cycle all the way back to denial, often numbing the pain with drugs, alcohol, television, or shopping.

If the forward movement can take place, the next stage, depression, can feel like the worst stage of all, but may be, in fact, the necessary step on the way to acceptance. Depression, often called anger turned inward, must be lived through, and the more quickly it can be accepted, honored, owned, and "worked," the better. People can get stuck in this stage of grief, as in all the others, forever.

In that hard, lonely process we call the grief process, we humans do go back and forth among the stages of grief, but my experience is that once a person makes that final surrender into authentic acceptance that says, "Would to God this had not happened. Would to God I had not been brought to this place, but having been brought here, I accept it for what it is."

Job did not merely resign himself to his situation. He did, in fact, fight and wrestle all the way to the mat of true acceptance, an acceptance that is made out of strength and courage.

What Job comes to accept in this terrible wrestling match is that the ways of God are inscrutable and that it is not possible for human beings to call the shots when it comes to relating to God. Indeed, God is, above all, autonomous. The wind of God's spirit really does blow where it will, and though we are made in the image of God, we are not God.

In accepting that his old ideas of God are not adequate for the present day's challenges, Job comes to accept the truth that while life does not any longer conform to his old ideas and that his way of being in the world no longer works, God's love is the constant that emanates throughout all of creation. Job comes to an inner knowing that he could not have as long as his focus is on the external world.

My own experience is that acceptance most often comes slowly, over time, and I admit that I probably delay the relief of it because I resist pain so habitually and fiercely. Over time, however, I have learned that whatever I resist persists.

I have learned that acceptance really is the key to serenity and it is what I do that gives God room to work. Even as I declare that, however, I have to admit that there have been those things that I, by myself, could not bring myself to accept, but as I have continued to turn my will and my life over to the care of God, God has worked at an unseen level of my mind and heart, just as I believe he did with Job, to bring about the acceptance that my stubborn will and proud ego could never accomplish.

Over time, I have come to be able to say more quickly, in the words of Dag Hammarskjold in *Markings*, "Thank you for all that has been" and "Yes . . . to what will be."

What must I give up, Lord?
What else?
What more do you want from me?

Down deep, in the places I
cannot see or know,
please pry the fingers of my resistance
from those things that
are keeping my soul bound
up in fear or anger, guilt or shame—
petty grievances and enormous grievings.

I'm pretty sure that,
as stubborn as I am,
there is still something

I'm holding on to,
clinging to it as if my
life depended on it—

and yet the
truth is
that my life really
depends on my
letting go
and letting you do whatever you
need to do.

And so, in this moment,
I surrender to you all of the things
that I know to surrender—

I let go of all
that I can—
and I trust you, Divine Therapist,
to work
deep in the
depths

to bring to my mind
that which I do not know—
to free me from the
bondage of my own will run riot—
to release me from the tyranny of my false self—
I surrender.
To your mercy, I surrender.
Into your love, I let go.

Chapter Thirteen

God in the Abyss

The cure for pain is in the pain.
—RUMI

*Pain was the loving and legitimate violence necessary
to produce my liberty.*
—PASCAL

Failure is the key to the kingdom within.
—RUMI

We are called to step into The Great Not Yet.
—JOHN CLAYPOOL

A young, popular minister steps into the baptismal waters in University Baptist Church in Waco, Texas, and reaches for the microphone. There, in front of hundreds of worshipers, including his wife, he is electrocuted.

What did he do to deserve that? And where was God in that horrible moment?

An adolescent girl is told that if she will pray "in faith," her daddy will be healed, but he dies anyway.

Who will be with her when she asks her hard questions? Will anyone be able to reach through her self-protection and give her what she needs?

I hold my four-year-old granddaughter while she mourns. Inside, I am crying too. "Why hasn't God answered my prayer?" she asks me, and I hold her closer and try to absorb her pain. There's not much I can say, actually, and so I do all I can to comfort and soothe her, and I promise that I will be with her. Inside, I'm battling with God myself; answering the prayer of a little girl seems to be something God would want to do!

I join a network of hundreds of friends of John Claypool as he battles one infection after another in his valiant battle against multiple myeloma, and then, suddenly, he is snatched from us, and together we grieve, forming a web of collective sadness and anger that he, so generous with his wisdom and his love, is taken from us. Somehow, those of us who have been touched by John through the years form a kind of Internet community, comforting each other and attempting to give hope and comfort to Ann, his wife, and Rowan, his son, even if we have never actually met them or each other!

As I live out my life within a faith community, as I write to bring hope to others, and as I travel, speaking about the love of God, I carry always in my conscious mind the reality that life is not fair. Prayers are not always answered as we want them to be answered, and the people we pray for don't always make the choices we want them to make.

*

One of the most annoying experiences I can remember from my adolescence was a "testimony service" in which someone would tell a story about how God had redeemed him from some pit of hell and, now, he was a free man.

It was annoying to me to hear those dramatic, colorful, and sometimes titillating stories because, as the preacher's daughter, my story was so squeaky clean and boring that it felt like a non-story. Faith, up to that point, had been so easy for me that I longed for one of those blinding, life-changing experiences that I could talk about.

No matter how "good" I was as a young person, however, somebody who had lived a wild and raucous life would come along and give a better testimony and get the attention of the church ladies.

Later, when my husband was in seminary, all of us who had walked the straight and narrow pathways would speculate about whether you had to have some terrible experience of sin in order to have a good testimony. I shudder now, thinking back to how shallow our understanding of the life with God really was.

Still later, I learned that if you live long enough, life will happen to you and you will likely experience or do something that will bring you to your

GOD IN THE ABYSS

knees. Sometimes it is the very things of which you are most proud that become the means God can best use to get you to the abyss.

At times, it is the very things you think you cannot bear to lose that are taken from you, and sometimes it is when you are trying to be most holy that you fall the lowest. Sometimes it is trying to be so pure and so proud of your purity that you do the most damage. Nearly always, when you're all puffed up with your own purity and pride, you actually do more damage than when you are authentic and real. There's something really distasteful about purity that has to shout and show off. Shining examples have a way of falling off their pedestals, one way or another. "Give me one good juicy drunk any day," a friend in AA told me, "to a self-righteous, pompous hypocrite."

"The higher they fly," my mother would say, "the flatter they fall."

"The brighter the light," Carl Jung said, "the darker the shadow."

*

In his autobiography, *Cash*, legendary country-western singer Johnny Cash (referred to as a "Baptist mystic" by his daughter, Roseanne) describes the day he jumped into the abyss. Years of drug and alcohol abuse, marital woes, and all of the accompanying troubles of his life led him to drive his Jeep to the Nickajack Cave on the Tennessee River.

A cave is often symbolic of a womb, but on this occasion, Johnny Cash intended that cave to be his tomb. He describes crawling back into the darkness with the lack of light being appropriate to the separation from God that he was experiencing. He calls it the "deepest and most ravaging of the various kinds of loneliness" he had ever felt.

Suddenly, though, in the depths of that place of absolute surrender to the darkness, he began to experience an inexplicable sensation of utter peace, clarity, and sobriety.

Johnny Cash tells that he came out of that tomb/womb/cave a new person and that, from there, he began the painful process of recovery and redemption. In what my friend Keith Herron calls a "crazy mixture of heart-felt spirituality and broken earthiness," the man in black became a light and a symbol of hope for millions of people who loved his music. But even more loved the man who was not afraid to show his humanity. Johnny Cash was a *good man*, for he partnered with God in loving the world God loves.

I love this story about Johnny Cash. I love to hear about the times when God breaks through and reveals himself in a way that is just enough to keep a person taking the next step.

*

My daughter Amy led me to a singer and a song on the CD *Million Year Old Man*. In the song "Fall," the singer seems to be saying that the only way up is down: "What if the highest destination / Wasn't up above at all / What if, to reach the highest place / You had to fall?"

And so we hear the stories of God's meeting Johnny Cash in the cave. We read the story of Job's leap into the darkness, and we ask ourselves, and sometimes we ask God, what it takes to experience that kind of life-changing transformation Cash describes.

I still do not believe that God causes our suffering, but he does allow us to experience whatever we need to experience in order to be made whole, and sometimes that experience is terrifying beyond words.

Indeed, sometimes people respond to losses and failures in ways that do not make them any more whole than they were, and sometimes people are more broken and fragmented than before. God gives us freedom to respond as we will, and sometimes we simply cannot take the pain.

Sometimes we are humiliated beyond anything we could imagine, often by our own hand, yet it is those experiences that can bring us to deep humility. It is in our humility that God works. It is terribly painful to fall from grace because of our own choices, but, even there, God can move redemptively.

Formed in a society that taught me that if I would give something, I could expect to get something back, I came to expect that if I take a leap into the abyss in some form of radical trust, I can expect some kind of response to my action!

When I turn things over to God, I expect him to act. I think that my yielding to his will should make it clear to him that I am ready for him to do for me what I need to have done. Sometimes, however, it seems to me that when I give something to God, he says, "I don't want it either!" and gives it back to me.

Or is it that I take it back?

Perhaps there is still a shred of misunderstanding in me that would make me think that my yielding to God is a coin in the exchange between us. Authentic giving up is yielding to the presence and action of God in such a way that I have no expectations of outcomes and no preconceived notions of what God will or will not do. And that feels like jumping off into the abyss.

Surrendering to God is not a bargaining chip. It is not a negotiation tool, nor is it a highly specialized spiritual manipulation for "very spiritual people." We do not know when we surrender what will come next, which makes surrender even more challenging and terrifying.

When it comes to the work of transformation, there are no guarantees about anything. If there were, surrender would not require radical, gut-wrenching trust. It is not faith when I set the agenda for how things will unfold once I've made my big leap of faith.

There is something powerful in Job's coming to the end of his conversation with his friends. In his silence, there is the sense that he is at the point of radical surrender. He has been broken, and his heart has finally been broken open. It is in that condition that the spirit of God can begin to work, but God does not always work in the way we hope or in the way we plan or even in the way God worked in Job's life.

Sometimes our surrender gives God the room he needs to do things that are truly wonderful, things we love. Sometimes God's plan is different from ours, and different in ways that we think we cannot bear, and we have no way of knowing when we make the leap into the arms of God what is going to happen.

We are called to take leaps of faith, but we don't get to determine what the net will be. We do not know the shape or the size of the abyss, and we do not have any way of knowing what is on the other side of the leap, but what we learn from Job and from others who have made that leap into the brilliant darkness of the Light is that God is there.

We pray for healing for our loved ones, and we stand in the mysterious reality that one person with a particular kind of cancer gets well and lives a long life, and the other person who is the same age, has had the same level of nutrition, and has every reason to survive, dies.

We look to the victories in catastrophic illnesses. We expect all our babies to be born perfect. We think that we can outrun the clocks of time, and yet we must remember that even the people Jesus healed did, finally, die.

*

Recently, my husband and I attended the funeral service of Phil Strickland, who for years stood for ethics and social justice for the Baptist General Convention of Texas, as the executive director of the Christian Life Commission. Martus and I had known Phil and his wife, Carolyn, for all of our adult lives. We had served on various committees with him, and had watched him live out his life as a champion of those who could not speak for themselves. We had also observed his valiant battle with cancer for over twenty years, one-third of his life.

Phil was not "cured," as we define cured. In spite of the multitude of prayers of hundreds of people, Phil was not "healed," as we understand healing. However, with our limited and finite vision, we cannot see on the other side of this life, and we don't know what the big picture is. What we see as loss may be, from a larger perspective, gain. What we understand as an ending, on this side of life, is a glorious beginning in a new dimension that we earthbound people cannot envision.

At the funeral service, George Mason, his pastor at Wilshire Baptist Church in Dallas, and our friend, described Phil as "a man of love" who showed us his scars. Mason read from an entry in Phil's personal journal, dated in 1998, eight years before he died.

> Reading the book of James, which starts out with the notion that one should welcome trials with anticipation. The reason being that difficulties can reshape a person like storms can reshape the land. And so it is. The contours of my conceptions are shifting. . . . The cancer is a force of change. And there is at least the possibility that I can let it draw me toward a deeper understanding of one simple truth—God, the creator and sustainer of all is real.

"If cancer was a test," continued George Mason, "Phil passed it." "It never defeated him, because God was more real than the cancer. He lived and loved to the last day."

And then, Mason asked, "What is the test of your life? Will you pass it? Phil would tell you that the secret is in knowing personally the God who is real, and trusting that God in all things."

Mason quoted the prophet Muhammad, a gesture to the connections and friendships Phil had formed outside his own faith community: "Let the scar of the heart be seen, for by their scars are known the men who are in the way of love."

*

As Job came to his moment of utter silence, and when the friends finally had said all they had to say, no one could have predicted what would happen next. We simply do not know what is going to happen to us on the other side of giving up. We do not offer our sacrifice of surrender with strings attached. We offer our whole lives to God, and then we wait some more.

Henri Nouwen, wounded and broken, wrote powerfully about the "wounded healer." One of the most influential Christians and teachers of the twentieth century, Nouwen wrote prolifically on the depth of prayer. A popular speaker and beloved priest, he described going back to his room after a speaking engagement and weeping, alone in his bed, and wishing that someone had asked him to go for coffee.

Jacob wrestled with the angel, the messenger from God. "I will not let go until you bless me," he told the angel, and after an all-night wrestling match, Jacob walked from that time on with a limp. Many of us limp, though others don't notice.

Johnny Cash bore the consequences of his abuse of his body in that body, and he bore the sorrows of those prisoners who never got to walk free.

Jesus put his life on the line with his outrageous ideas about love and forgiveness, and finally he offered up his own physical body on a criminal's cross. The human Jesus had to die in order for the resurrected Christ to be set free.

The leap into the abyss is not some sentimental journey in feel-good spirituality. It will likely be the hardest thing you will ever be asked to do.

You may be required to give up all that has given you security and comfort.

You may be required to surrender all that you have achieved, accomplished, and acquired.

You may be asked to give up a lifelong belief system and the accompanying habits and behaviors.

You may be asked to give up your favorite gods.

Whatever it is the abyss asks of you, it will feel like a death, and sometimes something must, indeed, die, and that very thing that must die may be any ideas you may have that you can manipulate God into doing for you what you want him to do.

*

On a warm summer day last June, Janet Dromgoole went out for a run on the streets of St. Louis, Missouri, and never came back. Janet, who was thirty-one, was getting ready for her upcoming wedding. She had a career she loved and family who loved her.

Janet died of mitral valve prolapse and an "enlarged heart," a condition that her family said perfectly expressed her personality, and she left a huge vacuum in her family's life.

Janet's sister, Jennifer, and her mother, Maggie Thomas, a longtime friend, and I have carried on a round robin correspondence, and Jennifer wrote last week words that inspire and encourage me:

It is the coarsest form of denial to believe that God will keep me from all difficulty in my life just because I am a Christian. It may even be idol worship if I form a god in my head who behaves that way. I hate Janet's early death. I wish we had her here. But since we don't, and we have to move forward without her, I feel it is absolutely necessary to move forward yielded to God and to what he would desire to bring out of this experience.

Maggie told me as she grieved, "Even as we join the ranks of the 'walking wounded,'" she said, "we can be assured God joins us in our sorrow and continues to care for us."

My writing studio is right in the middle of a busy commercial district of Houston, Texas, just two blocks north of one of the largest megachurches in the country. Between that building and my writing studio is a life-size Presbyterian church. Recently, a sign outside that Presbyterian church caught my eye and made me smile: "God is not your Sugar Daddy," it proclaimed.

I tell my children that there is no place they can go where God is not, and that God is in the deepest, darkest, scariest pit. I remind them that his love will pursue them to the farthest reaches of their lives and that God's love can heal and transform them, liberate and empower them. God's love will sustain them, no matter what—even when our most fervent prayers are not answered as we want them to be. God will never leave us. God will not forsake us.

God is not, however, a Sugar Daddy.

I'm not sure who it was that told me
to leap—to let

go of my symbols of
security and
                    take a chance,
        take a risk,

        give God a chance,

        step out of the boat,
trust and obey.

You won't know,
she said,   what God will do
as long as you're clinging to
those things that keep you
stuck.
                Well, no kidding!

Maybe it just isn't time yet,
she said, when it didn't turn
out like she told me it would.

Maybe you leaped too soon.
Maybe you weren't supposed to
        leap. Maybe you should have
waited a little longer—you know,
for things to work out in their own way.
                Yeah? You think so?
                Well, what now? WHAT NOW?
Wait!
I'll wait.
This time, I'm waiting. I'm going to listen for a different
                                                voice.
        God's first language, they tell me, is silence.

        I think I'll wait.
        I think I'll wait for the silence to speak.

Chapter   Fourteen

The Whisper of His Grace

In my deepest wound I see your glory, and it dazzles me.
—St. Augustine

One moment your life is like a stone in you, and the next, a star.
—Rainer Maria Rilke

*Last night, as I slept, I dreamt—marvelous error—
that it was God I had here in my heart.*
—Antonio Machado

On a warm fall afternoon, I left Methodist Hospital, in the heart of the Texas Medical Center, with the intention of going home to check the mail and then to purchase a dishwasher. My husband had had surgery for prostate cancer, and I was attempting to care for him and take care of things at home.

At the house, I checked my messages, and, to my dismay and heartbreak, there was a call from a friend, informing me that Sherry Holmes had died. I called Sherry's house immediately, spoke with one of the family members who took my cell phone number, and left in a rush to finish errands.

At the time, Main Street, which threads through the Medical Center to downtown Houston, was in shambles as workers were tearing up the streets and preparing the routes for the new Metro Rail System. The outer world of chaos and disorder mirrored my inner world of anxiety over my husband's health and, now, grief over Sherry's death.

I wondered if the family knew that my husband, their pastor, was in the hospital. I fretted about how I could help, and yet, somehow, I managed to get through the horrendous construction zones.

Somewhere in the midst of that chaos on Main Street, Ned Holmes, Sherry's husband, called me on my cell phone and said, "Jeanie, we want you to do the funeral service."

Negotiating through the heavy traffic and trying to avoid the construction barriers, I argued with Ned, telling him that I would help him find a man who could do the service. I reminded him that I was not "ordained," and he told me he didn't care. I gave him some more excuses, all born out of my own insecurities and my own anxiety about performing such a role in a church that had, only a few weeks before, voted down a motion to ordain women as deacons.

Finally, impatient with my excuses, Ned said, "Look, Jeanie, if you don't want to do it . . . "

I quickly said, "Ned, I'll do it."

With long years of living in a minister's home, I knew exactly what to do next. I made arrangements to see the family. I told him what I would need, and I asked the appropriate questions.

I do not remember much more from that point until I got to the Sears parking lot, somehow driving through the rubble and congested traffic to a safe parking place. Pulling in to that parking place, I put my head down on the steering wheel and wept. I wept for the loss of my friend. I wept over my husband's illness. And I wept in the face of God's flinging himself across my path, giving me an opportunity to do something important for my friend. It felt to me that God had broken through all of my resistance, and in that grace-filled moment, I could almost hear Sherry, with a touch of impatience in her voice, saying, "Come on. Get over it and get with it. You can do this."

On the day of Sherry's funeral, the weather was dark and gloomy and humid. The sanctuary that holds 450 people had to stretch to accommodate 700 mourners. Ushers filled the choir loft and latecomers had to stand, packed, in the hallway outside the sanctuary. The mayor and the former mayor crowded in to the pews alongside friends and family.

As much public speaking as I have done in the past twenty-five years, I was, nevertheless, nervous about this assignment, but not because of who was to be in attendance. It was that it was unusual and unprecedented for a woman to be in charge of a funeral that had me churning. But, even more, I so wanted to do a really good job for Sherry, who had done such a good job of giving me courage, and so I had written my friend, Nancy DeForest, and asked her to pray for me.

As I walked in and took my place in front of the chair on the podium, I was startled to see Nancy DeForest sitting directly behind the chair where I would sit. A priest at St. John the Divine Episcopal Church, she smiled at me, and I mouthed the words, "What are you doing here?"

All during the funeral, I could feel Nancy's strength behind me. Later, I sent her an e-mail, asking who she knew in the family. The Holmes family has lived in this area of Houston for decades, and there are numerous family members, so I assumed that she was a friend of part of the family.

"I don't know any of them," Nancy wrote back. "But you had asked me to pray for you, and so I decided that the best way to pray for you was to come and be with you. Who could have known that the sanctuary would be so full that I would have to sit in the choir loft, *right behind you.*"

Who, indeed!

Nancy's presence was a whisper of God's grace.

*

As I finished my tribute to Sherry, invoking in my sermon the life of Job and recalling how Sherry had drawn great strength from the study of Job, I built up to the last point of my message. In the hour that we had been there, the sky had become even darker.

"It was not only that Sherry was physically beautiful," I said, coming to my concluding remarks, " but that she radiated courage and optimism in the face of her illness and suffering."

I paused to swallow hard and compose myself, barely able to bear looking at the faces of Sherry's daughters, Erin and Allison, seated with their dad, recalling how deeply she loved her family.

Gathering my courage, I leaned into the podium for strength, but also wanting to be closer to the family.

"Sherry was," I continued, "*lit from within* by the grace of God," and at that precise moment, the sun came out from behind the thick clouds that had hung over Houston all day long and literally flooded that sanctuary with light! Chills ran over my body, and somehow I managed to get through to the end, but I wondered if anyone else noticed what had happened.

"I thought you had arranged that for dramatic effect," a friend wrote in a note, "and I even turned to see who had turned on the lights!"

It was not I who turned on the lights.

Was it God? Was it mere coincidence? Who else could it have been, flooding the sanctuary with lights at that precise moment? Was that a whisper of God's grace, a touch of mercy, a reminder of the presence of God?

*

Within a week, I rushed into Hungry's restaurant near Rice University to meet my family for lunch, and when I sat down at the table with them, I was startled by the brilliance of a painting that hung above our table. The painting was of a shaft of dazzling yellow light, breaking through darkness.

Speechless, I could not take my eyes off the painting.

"I can't believe you like that painting!" my husband said. "Those aren't the colors you like . . . and it's abstract. You don't even like abstract art!"

He was right. Up until that moment, I would no more have imagined liking that painting than I would have imagined delivering the sermon in my church. The painting, though, was a visual representation of what had happened to me that day on Main Street, when Ned called me and asked me to do something that was, for me, radical and outrageous, and then what had happened in the sanctuary at Sherry's funeral. God had broken through darkness in both instances, with light and life and love and laughter.

That—breaking through darkness with his marvelous light—is one of the things God does best.

Later, I met the artist, a lovely Muslim woman, who told me that she was at a low point in her own life, down in Puerto Rico with her only child who was moving out of the country. She had been so dispirited that she wouldn't even check her e-mails until her husband told her that she had to read mine, for I was inquiring about purchasing her painting.

Was God at work in both our lives, touching us with hope, whispering grace?

That painting hangs over the small altar in the apartment/studio where I write and do spiritual direction. Often, when a directee is struggling to discern the direction of the spirit of God in her life, I will call her attention to that painting and tell her the story, and we are both encouraged to wait until God breaks through our darkness, separating the light from the darkness and guiding us into the paths that have been hidden from us.

Daily, I look at that painting and remember that God, who has been with me in the past, has not left me and, in the appropriate moments and in his time, will break through my confusion or my doubts, my uncertainties and my darkness again, leading me out into his marvelous light.

THE WHISPER OF HIS GRACE

Johnny Cash intended for that deep, dark cave of his despair to be his tomb, but God had another idea. Instead of a tomb, that cave became a womb. God reached down into the darkness of the earth and the darkness of Johnny Cash's heart and shed his brilliant, healing, transforming light.

Jesus wrestled mightily with the evil one in the wilderness, and when he took his stand about what kind of Messiah he would be and how he would manifest his Father's will in bringing in the kingdom of God, the Scripture says that an angel attended to him.

"I am willing to keep on working through this problem," I proclaimed one day, "if I can know this is productive pain."

It's hard to know, sometimes, the difference between pain that is leading nowhere and the pain of labor that will birth something good, yet when you're in the middle of the pain, you have to keep on laboring with it with faith, however slight, that the pain will be productive.

If I had been Job, the appearance of the young upstart, Elihu, would have driven me to the end of my rope.

Where did this young kid come from, with all of his brashness and self-assuredness?

Did he think that he could do what the older friends could not do?

My daughter, Amy, in the last year of a four-year graduate program in social work and theology at Baylor University and Truett Seminary in Waco, went with her fellow graduate students to Austin to "march on the capitol." Carrying their protest signs, they chanted as they walked toward the capitol building: "What do we want? *Social justice!* When do we want it? *NOW!*"

"What does your generation not want now?" we teased her, and she, taking herself lightly, laughed with us, even as she took seriously her work in the issues of social justice in the name of God.

*

Perhaps Elihu stands as a symbol for something new that will break through in Job's experience. Perhaps in his boldness, he symbolizes new strength that will be born from within the depths of Job's own being. At the end of his speech, however, Job does not even respond.

I've noticed that I can end all dialogue with others when I lecture them instead of listen. I can shut the hearts and minds of my loved ones, and they mine, when I come from a place of superiority, talking down to them, shaming them, or pointing out their flaws. Even if what I say holds a kernel of truth, that kernel rarely sprouts if I've sown it and watered it with self-righteousness and criticism.

I admire Job for hanging in there throughout the "discourses" and for tolerating his friends. Along the way, however, there were those breakthrough moments when the spirit of the Living God spoke from within Job's own inner sanctuary, and I believe that it was those significant whispers of grace that gave him just the amount of strength and courage, stamina and perseverance, to sit strong.

Hanging on when you are caught in the depths of an impossible situation and cannot see your way out of it is one of the biggest challenges human beings face. Keeping the faith when neither option that is available to you is a good one requires unbelievable courage, and waiting on God when you feel trapped, with no way out, is sometimes an almost unbearable agony.

"Leap, and the net will appear," a popular refrigerator magnet, sounds good, unless you know that if you leap you are going to create even more trouble for yourself than you already have.

*

When we moved from San Angelo to Houston, Texas, in 1992, we moved into a new house in an area where the older houses were being torn down to make room for new houses. Two enormous pecan trees provided a canopy over our backyard. Coming from living for fourteen years in West Texas, we were thrilled with those trees and the lovely shade they provided.

In the winter months that followed our move, my father had died and my sisters and I had closed our family home and moved our mother to a retirement facility in Amarillo, Texas. In that bleak winter, many layers of grief accompanied me day after day.

One day, sitting in my den, I looked out at those lovely trees, bare and empty of leaves, and reminded myself that new life, though hidden, would spring forth from them in just a few weeks. Fresh, green leaves would push their way out of those barren limbs, and the lovely green canopy would cover our backyard and shade the windows along the back of the house again. The promise of those leaves was a symbol of hope for me.

What I had no way of knowing in that deep, dark winter of grieving was that, in the construction process of our house , something had happened to the root system of those old pecan trees. Even as I held on to hope, our trees were dying.

Sometimes life is like that, and the scary thing is that as you participate in life, fully engaged with the cycles of life that pervade every living thing, you don't always know if something has died or if the life force is just resting, waiting for the right moment to emerge again.

To "get off the ash heap" too soon is to sabotage the work of God. To seize control of a situation instead of letting it unfold, to leap before it is time, to act too quickly to relieve the pain is to miss the blessing that is embedded, albeit out of sight to the human eye, in the pain. To interfere with what God is trying to do is to play God and, often, to make matters worse.

All along Job's journey, there are moments when God breaks through into Job's consciousness in such a new way that, I believe, Job is given just what he needs to keep on sitting strong until the work of God in Job is fully accomplished.

Driven to frustration by the first round of discourses, God broke through to Job, speaking clearly in his agony, recorded in Job 19:20-29. Surely these words, a comfort for generations of suffering people, are evidence of God's presence with Job on that ash heap. Surely this whisper of God's grace is from God to Job, intended to aid him in his suffering:

> I know that my Redeemer lives, and that in the end he will stand upon the earth. And after my skin has been destroyed, yet in my flesh I will see God. I myself will see him with my own eyes—I , and not another. How my heart yearns within me.

*

In the fall of 2005, it was my privilege to speak on the reality of God's presence in prayer at a conference, "Beside Still Waters," at Bonhomme Presbyterian Church in St. Louis, Missouri.

On the first night, I attended a dinner in the home of members of the committee that put together the conference, and in getting acquainted with one of the committee members, I was stunned to hear her tell about the murder of her daughter. Haunted by the account of the young woman's brutal killing at the hands of people she was attempting to help, I related to this mother that I was working on a book on the book of Job.

On Sunday morning, I was to deliver the sermon, which I had titled "The Whisper of His Grace." As I sat behind the pulpit, collecting my thoughts and calming my own nerves, I looked across the chancel and smiled at the woman, a member of the choir, who had told me her story on Friday night before the conference.

Suddenly, looking at the worship guide, I realized that it was she who was going to be singing the solo "I Know That My Redeemer Lives," right before I was to deliver the sermon.

Before I could fully process the impact of this holy, precious moment, she stood up, and with perfect poise and in the voice of an angel, she sang out her proclamation of faith in the community of faith that had held her and sustained her and nourished her in the dark days of her grief.

When she sat down, I was trembling, and I thought that surely she must be as well. Our eyes met, and I put my hand on my heart and mouthed the words, "Thank you. *Thank you!*"

Encouraged by the witness of God's redemptive love at work in the darkest of circumstances, I stood up to deliver my sermon. Little did I know that the very next week, I would call on her faith and Job's witness to the Living Redeemer as my family entered a new season of illness.

God is always at work in seen and unseen ways, and it is often at the point of our extremity that we most need to stop and listen for the whispers of his grace. Sometimes God is at work in the endings of things, and sometimes in the birthings of things. But, always, God is at work, attempting to bring about good.

*

When my oldest daughter, Michelle, called our house early in the morning hours on Holy Saturday in 2001, I leapt to the phone. She told us that she was in labor, and needed me to come immediately to be with her.

On the flight from Houston to Lubbock, Texas, my prayers were mingled with excitement over the birth of my first grandchild and anxiety for my own child. I had concerns that she, like I, would labor long and then, because of her physical structure, deliver quickly, catching the doctors off-guard.

Sure enough, when I got to the hospital, she was progressing in precisely the way that I had. Her labor pains were intense and close together, but they weren't productive. Knowing that it was a holiday weekend and that this was not her doctor, I feared that the doctor would push for a Caesarean section too soon. Soon, the doctor who was on call came into the birthing room and told Michelle that she might have to have a Caesarean shortly.

I walked over to her bed and looked straight into those gorgeous, dark brown eyes and said, "Michelle, you must do what is best for you and for your baby, but *I think you can do this!*"

The labor room nurse, who was at least ten feet tall, was checking the monitor as I said that, and when I left the room, she said, "Who was that?" and my daughter said, "My mother." I've never asked what tone of voice either of them used, but later Michelle told me that the nurse said to her, "I think you can do this too."

THE WHISPER OF HIS GRACE

I stepped outside the birthing room and called my husband and daughter, Amy, who were in Houston, almost beside themselves with excitement over the birth of this baby, our first grandchild and the first niece for Amy and Julie. My son-in-law came out of the birthing room and said, "We're going to have a baby. I'll tell you later what the nurse did," and within ten minutes I heard the most beautiful cry in the world, the protest of my first grandchild, Abby, who had made her first difficult journey from the quiet, warm, and safe womb of her mother to a world filled with light and sound, smells and sensations.

Later, my daughter told me that after I left the room, the labor room nurse had rolled Michelle over on her side and had made her pull her legs up, contorting that laboring woman into a strange and miserable position.

Telling my longtime friend John Jennings about what had happened, he laughed. A lifelong obstetrician and head of the OB/GYN residency program at the University of Texas Medical School in Galveston, John said, "That's the pretzel move, and what it does is tilt the pelvis *just a fraction*, but the small fraction is just enough that the baby can move down into the birth canal."

*

Sometimes all God needs is just the slightest movement on our part. Sometimes all we need to endure the long, hard waits of our lives is just one small whisper of grace.

Sometimes, when we least expect it, and sometimes in ways that are invisible to the eye of those who refuse to see, inaudible to the ears of those who will not hear, and unknowable to those whose hearts are closed, God moves in mysterious ways and performs, one more time, a miracle.

In reciting some of the mighty acts of God, Job says, "And these are but the outer fringe of his works. How faint the whisper we hear of him! Who then can understand the thunder of his power?" (Job 26:14).

In my own journey, I have learned that if you will wait in the darkness long enough, you will come to see that the Light has been there all along.

I have learned, in enduring the unbearable sense of God's absence, that there is no place I can go where God is not, and in the places where the seeming absence of God is unbearable, God is present, fully.

I have learned that if I will sit in the silence of God long enough, bearing that silence and waiting for what sometimes feels like an eternity, eventually I will hear the singing of God, the sounds of God, the love of God.

God whispers constantly, and the whisper is within the innermost chambers of the human heart, where God is at home.

Ah! Sometimes you take my breath away,
    gracing a moment with some
      new color in the sky
or the unexpected
call from a friend
just at the right moment.

        Sometimes you play the trickster,
    making me laugh,
    giving me riddles,
      sending me dreams,
    sneaking up on my blind side
      and surprising me,
          turning clowns upside down, and
            speaking of holy things in common vessels.

Sometimes you are so bold
that I can't miss that it's you,
    but often
you are hidden in
plain sight, and I don't realize
what I've seen or heard or
felt until
    I wake up the next morning
      and realize an ordinary moment in my day had your
signature
    written all over it.

      Grant me sharper eyes to
      see your fingerprints,
      better hearing to
      hear your whispers of grace,
        more highly tuned senses
      so that I can feel your small mercies.

      Your grace really is
      amazing, and it does
come softly.
      Please, God, don't let me miss your whisper!

God Is the Verb

You touched me—and the world didn't change—but I began to. . . .
You touched me—and since you did, I haven't been the same.
—MARILEE ZDENEK

Earth is crammed with heaven, and every common bush afire with
God, but only he who sees takes off his shoes.
—ELIZABETH BARRETT BROWNING

As I write this, I know that in only a few days, the wildflowers of Texas will begin pushing through the earth, setting entire fields ablaze with color. Bluebonnets, our state flower, will paint the hillsides blue, and families will stop along the highways to take pictures.

In my collection of photographs, one of my favorites reveals the magnificent fuchsia wildflowers that had pushed their way up through the hard, grim, gray concrete of so desolate a place as the prison at Alcatraz. Another of my favorites is a picture of small, delicate yellow flowers clustered in the cracks of an ancient stone wall in a small English village.

I fuss about technology and how hard it is for me to keep current with a computer and how paralyzed we are when some aspect of our world shuts down because "the computer is down." However, when I remember the relief we had when a prenatal sonogram of our grandson, Matthew, revealed that he was, after all, healthy, I chide myself for fussing about the occasional breakdowns of technology.

In the year 2004, each of my daughters had a baby within five weeks, and I noticed that having babies was really "in" among their peers. It seemed to me that that burst of babies following the attacks on our country in September of 2001 was almost a fist in the face of that which would thwart life itself. To me, so many babies all at once was an affirmation of hope, a reminder from God that the world would go on, at least for now.

What is this force of life that pulsates throughout creation if not the work of God? What is it that makes people keep on composing music in spite of how many songs have been composed, sung, and recorded? What makes people keep on designing beautiful houses of worship even though religion is fraught with conflict and peril? What makes young couples continue to make plans and make babies in the face of terrorism, tsunamis, war, and rumors of war?

What is it that keeps hope alive in a world that sometimes seems to be conspiring to keep us feeling hopeless and helpless?

What is it that makes a yearling suddenly decide to stand up and walk, and no matter how many times she falls, she keeps on standing up and putting one foot in front of the other?

What is it that makes scientists keep on searching for a cure for disease? And what is it that makes parents keep on praying for their lost and lonely children?

What makes people decide to get up in the morning and take on the heroic task of caring for their daily responsibilities in the face of unbelievable difficulty and, now and then, even danger? What makes people stay alive and vibrant, carrying on with hope in the face of the mundane and the mind-numbing routines of their lives? It is, indeed, awe-inspiring when persons do not give in either to their terrors or the human tendency to lethargy. What a victory over fear it is when people suit up and show up, daring to live and declaring, "I'm in! I'm a player! You can count on me!"

I believe it is the life of God at work in us, which animates all of creation, that keeps us doing what we must do and can do. That energy of God, that very life force, the force Dylan Thomas calls "the force that through the green fuse drives the flower," was alive in my friend Sherry, driving her to fight for her life, and yet it was that same dynamic mystery that transitioned Sherry to the next phase of her journey, on the other side of this life.

*

When Job had said all he could say, and when the friends were rendered speechless, finally, God spoke. I have noticed that God often waits until we humans have exhausted ourselves to speak. I have observed that it is, as my father told me, "often darkest right before the dawn."

God spoke in his own time and in his own way, but he did not answer the why questions. He does not justify what happened to Job or his part in it. To our utter chagrin and irritation, God does not give reasons why he let Satan have his way with Job. *God Almighty does not explain his behavior.*

And to make matters worse, God says to Job , "I am the one who will question you!"

Indeed, God questions all of us, and the questions are pretty much the same:

> *Do you trust me?*
> *Do you love me?*
> *Will you love me no matter what?*
> *Where are you?*
> *Who do you say that I am?*
> *Do you want to get well?*

We can wrestle, argue, and probe. We can question and theorize, postulate and ponder, but in the end, it really is God who questions us, and how we answer shapes our lives. The truth is that we don't get to put God on the witness stand. We don't put God on retainer, calling him in when we need him and then excusing him when it suits our purposes to do so.

*

God's speech to Job reminds me of two of my favorite quotes, quotes that keep me remembering that God is, after all, the Creator and that I am, indeed, the creature.

> *"The only thing you need to know about God is that you ain't he."*
> *"You can dance with God . . . but you have to let him lead."*

God answers Job, not with reasons that will satisfy his why questions nor a justification of his actions, but more with a testimony of who he is. In the end, God draws near to Job with his holy presence, and that is the answer that matters.

Job is never given a reason for his suffering and his losses. He is confronted, instead, by a new realization of God's presence. It is intrinsic to the nature of God that God will remain, of all things, mystery, and his ways, mysterious.

Sadly, we human beings are, for the most part, resistant to that which is mysterious, often calling it strange or weird. We prefer that which we can hold and manipulate, and yet God works in ways outside our control and manipulation.

We are a culture that insists on reasons and logic. We are bound to what we can explain rationally and to what is pragmatic and practical, and if we cannot explain something in our own terms, we may decide it isn't real. We are suspicious of anything that we cannot count, graph, or control, and we are especially afraid of the rich world of feeling, and yet the dynamic mystery of God moves as it will throughout creation.

My father used to say, "Don't be so open-minded that your brains fall out," expressing a kind of practical wisdom. He knew that wherever there was the possibility of great mystery or the work of the supernatural, there were often those who would exploit the mysterious and use it for a purpose for which it was not intended. There has always been a fine line between genius and insanity, mystery and quackery, the manifestations of the Spirit and simple acting out.

I wonder just how God spoke to Job. Did Job hear God as a large voice, speaking out of that whirlwind, or did God speak within the private chambers of Job's heart and mind? Did the friends hear the voice of God, or was this conversation for Job alone?

However God communicated with Job, God turned Job's attention away from his own plight and his questions to the wonders of the world, perhaps to broaden his vision, but also to reconnect him with his instinctual life. Perhaps God was helping Job to get himself off his own hands and see a larger world, the natural world, which is full of strange beasts that seem to serve no practical purpose.

God seems to remind Job that there is a larger world than his personal world and that God is at work in the midst of all of creation. God is out there, in all of creation, but God is also now in the heart of Job, speaking to him in language Job can understand.

Richard Rohr suggests in his book *Job and the Meaning of Suffering* that Job's suffering was the necessary pruning that led him to know that he was not separate from God. Job's was "a process of a lifetime, a movement toward union that will always feel like a loss of self-importance and autonomy."

It is my experience that the journey of life is intended to be the journey toward the life-altering realization that we are always in the presence of God and that God is always present to us. Sometimes it does take an entire lifetime to understand and accept this inalterable truth: God is with us. We are not ever apart from God, except in our consciousness. Separation from God is, in fact, impossible. Any sense of separation is an illusion.

"If I know God is with me, I can do this," a friend said to me when she was facing a hard experience. "It is the feeling of being alone and separate from God that terrifies me." Only going into that feeling and testing the limits of that perception would cure the feeling of separation.

*

Several years ago, while leading a retreat for the women of St. Luke's United Methodist Church in Houston at the beautiful Round Top Retreat Center in Round Top, Texas, I noticed an unusually beautiful and simple silver bracelet on the wrist of Chris Harris, one of the participants in the retreat who has become a dear friend. The lettering on it intrigued me, and I asked if I could see the bracelet. Chris eagerly took off her bracelet and let me read the words: "And lo, I am with you always."

I smiled because the memory of my father's reading the passage that includes this verse from John 14, his voice clear and confident, his back straight and strong, popped into my mind. Of all the passages I remember his reading during my childhood and adolescence, no passage had more of an impact than this one.

"My sister Carol gave that to me when I was going through a hard time," she told me. I admired the beautiful lettering on the bracelet and handed it back to her.

The next time I led a retreat for that particular group of women, I spotted the bracelet again, and again I asked to see it. I had an idea of some of the "hard times" this woman had experienced, and she mentioned that the bracelet was a little more worn than before.

Returning to Houston, I went to the James Avery store and purchased one of the bracelets for one of my daughters, with the intent of taking it to her the next week. Before I went, however, I decided that I needed one as well, and then I had to purchase bracelets for my other two daughters. What better message could I give to my children than the assurance of God's presence with them?

I wear my bracelet daily as a reminder of God's presence with me, and sometimes, when I am anxious or afraid, I run my fingers over the letters, carved into the silver. There's nothing magic or mystical about the bracelet or my wearing it, but there is something powerful about being reminded that, no matter what, God is with me, active and purposeful, accomplishing what God intends to accomplish. Like Lance Armstrong's yellow bracelets that encourage the wearer to "live strong," my bracelet reminds me to *sit strong* in the presence of God, who never leaves me, and to attempt to cooperate with the spirit of God.

"There's no place you can go where God is not," I tell my daughters, and we laugh, remembering that, as adolescents, that wasn't always good news!

*

Another of my bedrock Scriptures that forms the foundation of my life and my theology comes from Deuteronomy 30:19: "I have set before you today life and death, blessing and curse. Therefore, choose life."

Not only is God with us, but God is in us, somehow, and in us in a way that gives life. God is the power and force within us that moves us toward creativity and relationship, toward wholeness and transformation. God's spirit, dwelling in us, is the part of us that chooses life.

This God, who was alive in Job and who spoke with Job, is alive in all of creation, not as a fixed, concretized old man in the sky, but as the creative, vivifying, animating force, pulsing throughout creation.

As best I can understand God with my finite mind, and still with a determination not to attempt to define God, I understand God best as a verb. I understand God best as the healing, transforming, liberating, and empowering action of God in all of creation, moving, dynamic and alive, in the world. I understand God best as energy, and that energy is about unconditional love, grace, and mercy, set loose in the world.

Marilee Zdenek and Marge Champion express what I sense of God in his conversation with Job, and in my own life, from their book *God Is a Verb*:

> You are the healing
> The loving
> The touching
> You are the laughing
> You are the dancing
> Jesus, Verb of God
> You are the moving—
> Move in me.

Several years ago, during a question-and-answer period at a retreat, a participant asked, "How do you discern the will of God in prayer?"

The other retreat leader had a learned and lengthy response, which, thankfully, gave me time to refine my thoughts to a succinct and brief response.

"I try to follow the energy," I said, surprising myself, for I had never articulated that thought before. "And the energy is about life and love and, often, laughter."

Leaving the conference center that night, I realized that the answer that had come to me, unbidden and delightful, was guidance for me.

As part of our nature as creatures made in the very image of the Divine One, we are given the awesome privilege and terrible burden of choosing. When we choose to align ourselves with the creative power of the universe and the Creator and when we embrace our whole selves, when we live in consciousness and radical cooperation with the capacity to choose life, we are then able to be fully human and fully engaged with life in all of its fullness. Then, by our conscious choices, we participate with God in bringing in the kingdom of love.

I've always had trouble with the epilogue of Job because, in my world, people can go through terribly painful experiences and things are not restored and they don't get better, and in some cases they get worse.

Sometimes, when there is restoration, one person's profit is bought on the back of another's devastation. There are times when one group's gain is at the expense of another's loss, and there are those situations in which people never recover from what life has given them.

It bothers me when a person whose house was spared the ravages of a tornado when her neighbor's house was destroyed declares that "God spared us." What must the neighbor be thinking about God, I wonder.

I've always wondered what happened to the first Mrs. Job, and I've always read and taught this last part with disclaimers because the ending is just a little too perfect.

Again, the temptation is to look on outward "success" as the sign of God's blessing. At the risk of questioning the writers of the story, I have to caution against using this story to proclaim to others that if a hurricane has destroyed their home or taken their job, God has a better one waiting for them!

It does make a lot of sense to me, however, to interpret that epilogue not as a literal statement of Job's restoration, but as symbolic of the transformation that can happen when a person is faithful in the refiner's fire.

In fact, there is an interpretation that the book of Job is all a description of an inner process. Instead of the friends being actual men, they were voices of Job's inner complexes, parts of himself that he needed to face, and his crisis

173

was the crisis of midlife. Instead of his losing everything that was dear to him, everything that was dear to him somehow lost its meaning, and in his heroic struggle with his inner accusers, he came out of his wilderness experience in a completely new relationship with everything in his outer world.

However it happened, I do know that one of God's gifts in the refiner's fire is that when you have been through the transformation process, *everything is changed.* Everything becomes infused with a sense of God's presence. You see God's fingerprints more clearly and frequently and more consistently. Every exchange of persons carries the possibility of meeting God in the other. Every moment is potentially sacred because God is present.

*

Last Christmas, my daughter Amy gave me the song "Holy Now" on a CD, written and sung by Peter Mayer. Listening to the words as I traveled across Texas to lead a retreat at Laity Lodge, I played the song over and over. From the whirlwind of the past year, God spoke to me through the words of the song. Or, perhaps, it was God singing to me.

> So the challenging thing becomes
> Not to look for miracles
> But finding where there isn't one
> 'Cause everything is holy now.
> Everything is holy now.
> Everything . . . everything . . . everything is
> Holy now.

And yet. And yet. The presence of God does not guarantee that all will be smooth sailing. In fact, sometimes the very presence of God is that which pushes again and again out into deep waters, out onto the razor's edge of risk or into the unknown.

One day I made a comment to a friend that I would just like a little peace, for crying out loud! As a reward for my faithfulness, I confess, I wanted a break from the rigors of the too-much and the not-enough.

"There is no peace in peace," he said, shaking his head and grimacing.

"What are you talking about?" I demanded of him, but in my mind, I was hearing the words of Jesus, "I did not come to bring peace, but a sword." I could almost hear Jesus saying, "My peace I give you, not as the world gives," and suddenly I realized that what I was wanting was rest and respite, relief and deliverance, but that was not peace.

"Don't you know that hymn?" he asked me, and later he gave me a copy of the simple and profound hymn "The Christian Life," which describes what happened to "such happy simple fisherfolk before the Lord came down" in one verse and, in another, the fate of young John, known as the "the one Jesus loved," who died, homeless, on the Isle of Patmos, and Peter, the Rock, who died head down.

Indeed, peace is not the absence of conflict, but the presence and action of God in the midst of life, and where God is, there is sometimes comfort and sometimes confrontation. Where God is at work, there is sometimes a deep calm and confidence, and sometimes a divine restlessness. And where God is, love is, and love demands and implores, challenges and chastens, not letting go until, somehow, things are made whole.

It was the Prince of Peace who disturbed the peace of his own people, and for those of us who attempt to be his follower, we will likely be disturbed and disoriented. The hard, unvarnished truth is that the more deeply one goes into the heart of the Living Christ, the more likely one will be at odds with the culture.

The more fervently you pursue a relationship with Christ, the more that relationship will demand of you. Every times you think that you have come to a resting place, that stage of faith where you would like to camp out will be challenged, and the longer you walk with Christ in a sincere effort to abide in him, and he in you, the bigger challenges you will face. The real world of intimacy with Christ will turn what other people call "the real world" upside down and inside out, and you can count on that. After all, what is faith for if not to make a difference in your own personal world and the larger world?

The peace of Christ is not about lying on a flowery bed of ease, trouble-free.

It is, in fact, just about the most troubling thing I know, and it may be the most important peace worth pursuing.

I sing this song written by William Alexander Percy as my own prayer:

The peace of God, it is no peace,
But strife closed in the sod.
Yet let us pray for but one thing—
The marvelous peace of God.

God, Holy Autonomy and Living Verb, is alive in creation, making peace. That peace, however, does not always conform to our ideas of peace!

Holy Presence, Living God—
You are, Holy Verb,
    alive, dancing in all things.
        I cannot escape you, nor would I want to . . . now . . .
now that I've seen you, dancing.

Now that I've seen you, you seem to be everywhere.
Now that I've heard your whisper, I hear you more often.
Now that I have known your presence, I am no longer alone.
    And I am not so afraid.
    You are with me.
        You really are in all things.

But did I have to experience your absence to know this?
    Was all of that loss necessary to come to this fullness?

I know now that I do not have to beg you.
    I do not have to assault the heavens
        for you to hear me.
    I do not have to plead with you,
        for you cannot be absent from me.

You are the beloved, and you make me beloved.

I see now what was there all along.
    It was my blindness that made me see,
    my woundedness that made me know,
    my lostness that found you.

Now I am found.
I'm found in you.

Chapter Sixteen

Choose Life

I know . . . that my Redeemer lives.
—Job

I have come that you might have abundant life.
—Jesus of Nazareth

Clearly, psychological or spiritual development always requires a greater capacity in us for the toleration of anxiety and ambiguity. The capacity to accept this trouble state, abide it, and commit to life, is the moral measure of our maturity.

God cannot bring us to a new level of faith without challenging our present one.
—Thomas Keating

The ending of Job bothers me as much as the beginning because, in my experience, people are not always restored. Sometimes things do work out better than before, and there are occasions when the new order is infinitely better than the old one.

The world I live in is more often a Humpty Dumpty world and when Humpty Dumpty falls, he cracks into a million pieces, and no matter how many powerful people there are to put him back together, it can't happen.

The ending troubles me because of the first Mrs. Job. I can't keep from wondering what happened to her.

The reality is that we live in a world where one person's restoration is sometimes bought at the expense of another's devastation. One culture's victory is bought at the expense of another's defeat, and one person's gain is often on the back of someone else.

Again, to interpret this story literally is, I believe, to trivialize it, and that includes the ending. Perhaps the ending is best understood as the story of a man who, like the prodigal son, came to his senses and began to live in the world in a new way. Perhaps his heart had been broken open so that God no longer was "out there" but "in here."

Perhaps Job had gone through the wrenching, terrible process of egocide so that his false self was dismantled in order to let the true self live.

Kahlil Gibran says that "the deeper sorrow carves into our being, the more joy we can contain." Now Job could live from that place of deep, inner joy, the joy of knowing God, who dwells within the deepest place of the heart.

Maybe Job's outer life began to change because his inner life changed. Perhaps, above all, the book of Job is the story of an inside job. Perhaps Job was now motivated not by a desire to look good and have power, but to do good from a heart that had been softened and "tenderized."

Even if our stories do not turn out as we want them to, we can still choose life.

*

For ten years, Sherry Holmes sat near the front of a weekly Bible study I facilitate at the church my husband pastors in Houston. Sherry told people that I was her teacher.

As Sherry faced two devastating cancers, her consistent and quiet presence and her positive attitude profoundly affected all of us. She didn't talk about her suffering; she simply lived a radical faith week after week.

We who shared life with her continued to be amazed that Sherry didn't complain, and when she died, many in the Bible study said, "I had no idea she was sick!" When we who were her friends remarked to her that she was an inspiration to us, she was surprised. Seemingly, she was as oblivious to her amazing strength and grace as she was to her physical beauty and her impact on her friends.

I was deeply honored and scared to death to meet the challenge of delivering the sermon at Sherry's funeral, but as I prepared for it, I was thunderstruck by the realization that during the last four years, I might have been the designated teacher on Thursday mornings, but the truth is that *it was Sherry who was the real teacher.*

Indeed, in this mysterious dance between and among human beings, there is no true meeting of persons without each being affected and often transformed. In the encounter of one soul with another, both are impacted, and we are especially impacted by the suffering of our loved ones. In the authentic give-and-take between teacher and student, parent and child, husband and wife, friend and friend, something powerful, mysterious, and often numinous happens to both so that they both become both student and teacher.

Sherry taught me a lot about choosing life and blessing even in the midst of what does not work out and what is seemingly unbearable.

*

Sherry taught me that God's ways are not our ways. She and the prophet Isaiah understood that deep, perplexing truth. Sometimes it takes a very long time to discern the ways of God, and sometimes we get confused about what is God and what is not God. Perhaps we need to help each other more in learning better the ways of God so that we can cooperate with God more fully.

When God finally spoke to Job, he did not answer Job's or the friends' questions, and he did not justify his actions. Instead, he said, "I am the One who will question you." God continues to question us, and how we respond shapes our lives.

We so easily forget that God sees the big picture, and we see only a part of it. We who are so good at doing so many things are so prone to think that it is our job to tell God how to run the world. When we run headlong into our limitations or into that which we cannot understand or fix or change or control, and when we are staring into the barrel of our frailties and the dead end of our ability to tease life into being like we want life to be, we can either turn our backs on God and become bitter, or we can allow our suffering to expand our view of who God is.

We can either run from our troubles or we can, like Job, sit with them until we come to the place of knowing that we have put God in a box, often the size of our earliest childhood image of God. We can either resist life and its inevitable difficulties, or we can hold our problems, standing under them until we understand them.

The ineffable mystery that is God will not be reduced to a set of rules and rituals, definitions and dogmas. Suffering grants us the possibility of experiencing the grace of coming to know the goodness of God. Suffering will, if we allow it, introduce us to a far bigger and grander and more loving God than we could ever have imagined. And suffering, if we can bear it and wait in the anguish long enough, will refine us and convince us that God's will toward us is always good.

Our fear is that we do not know when we go into the fire of suffering, whether we will come out silver or cinder.

While Sherry's life on this plane ended, she was refined by her suffering.

One of my favorite songs, sung by the Dove Award-winning singer Cynthia Clawson, tends my heart and soothes my uneasiness. Its simplicity is childlike, but not childish: "God is too wise to be mistaken / God is too good to be unkind / And when you can't see his hand / When you don't understand . . . trust his heart.

*

Sherry taught us that God is at work in all things, attempting to bring about good. Perhaps God moved Job's attention to the natural world to get him to look beyond his own suffering and his own concerns to see the bigger picture of life all around him. Maybe God was attempting to reconnect Job to the natural world and his instinctual life. Maybe he was working to get Job out of his head and into nature.

God is found in the mundane and the ordinary, and sometimes God is even hidden in the profane. Indeed, sometimes a loss as severe as the death of a loved one often feels like profanity, but when you know that God is love and that God is good, in the truest sense of the word, it is easier to trust in the darkness.

We can and we must grieve when we lose that which is vital and precious to us, and Job teaches us that we can rail against the things that wound and afflict us. Indeed, deep loss is worthy of our tears, and if we do not dry our tears, we will pay. This kind of loss must be given the honor it is due. We must grieve well in order to heal well.

We can and we must ask our hardest questions of God, but in the end we will find, just as Job did and just as Sherry did, that the why questions leave us chasing ourselves around in circles that get us nowhere we want to go. My experience is that all of the reasons in the world won't make us feel any better when we lose a loved one.

It is Job, out of the agony and the anguish of the ash heap, who teaches us that at the end of our questioning, it is not why that matters but Who we encounter in the midst of our heartache. I saw in Sherry that God was with her in the depths of the deepest valley. Surely, Sherry heard the whisper of God's grace, as Job did, for what we saw in her was uncommon grace.

Sherry stood up to her illness and she fought to live, but she was able to handle what life had handed her with a dignity and grace that stand as a challenge to all of us who knew her. Sherry was transformed by her suffering, and we who experienced Sherry's suffering were transformed as well by what happened to her.

We cannot have watched Sherry and not face our own difficulties better. She set for us a benchmark, and I tremble before her example.

*

Sherry showed us that God invites us to choose life, and to choose it day by day. By thousands of small choices across a lifetime and by a few major choices, we can say "Yes" or "No" to life and to the invitation of God to participate with him in the adventure of life. How we respond to the invitations of God shapes our lives and the lives of others.

On a hot July day, I stepped off the elevator on one of the floors at M. D. Anderson Hospital just in time to see a flash of royal blue attached to an IV pole, speeding down the hall. It was my friend, Sherry Holmes, and she was doing laps around the hallways.

When I could finally catch her, she embraced me warmly and we returned to her room to visit. Sherry was hooked up to countless tubes, and as we talked, she poked fun at the contraption that covered her nose. "I look like an elephant," she joked, "with this thing on my nose." Actually, she looked beautiful.

In the course of the conversation, Sherry said, "This cancer is finally going to get me. There is no cure for this cancer, and I know it, but I'm going to fight it as long as I can." There was no self-pity in her tone or her words. What I heard was a calm acceptance of facts and a fierce determination to make the most of her life in the present moment.

What was it except for the life of God in her that kept Sherry fighting?

On my desk sits a brass paperweight in the shape of the Hebrew symbol of "life!" It reminds me of my bedrock Scripture and my conscious decision to say "Yes!" to the invitations of God.

By our choices, day by day, we are choosing life or death, blessing or curse, and the more conscious we are, the more choice we have. We choose, day by day, to live our lives as if to a funeral dirge, a military drill, a frenzied heavy metal rock song, or a graceful dance.

To choose life means that we choose to partner with God in co-creating life. We participate with God in his redemptive work in all of life.

We choose to live our *own* lives, not the life someone else has chosen for us.

We choose to live as people made in the image of God, living up to the high calling that is ours or, as Jim Hollis calls it, "the largeness of our lives."

We choose life by doing what we were sent here to do, fully engaged with life and as participants instead of observers in the great drama of life. We are givers and not takers, though we understand that we must receive from others and from God.

We choose life by seeking the truth, living the truth, and telling the truth. Refusing to hide in denial, we face our sorrows and our losses with the understanding that God is at work in all things, attempting to bring about good.

We choose life by choosing to be people of hope and by making peace where we can and as we can.

We choose life by living as lovers in the world, loving God and loving people, loving life and the life you have been given, loving your own fate and even your own flaws.

And we choose life, knowing that much of the time, certainty is uncertain, risk is a guarantee, and not all landings will be smooth and easy. I keep a copy of Thomas Merton's prayer with me at all times so that when I get nervous about what I'm doing, I can let go of the nervousness and trust the One who is with me:

> My Lord God, I have no idea where I am going. I do not see the road ahead of me. I cannot know for certain where it will end. Nor do I really know myself, and the fact that I think that I am following your will does not mean that I am actually doing so. But I believe that the desire to please you does in fact please you. And I hope I have that desire in all that I am doing. I hope that I will never do anything apart from that desire. And I know that if I do this you will lead me by the right road though I may know nothing about it. Therefore will I trust you always, though I may seem to be long and in the shadow of death. I will not fear, for you are ever with me, and you will never leave me to face my perils alone.

Sherry taught us again that love is the most powerful force in the world. In the end, it was her family who mattered most to her. The people she had loved were of ultimate importance to her. In a note she wrote to her family, she got down to the most important things:

> My precious family—I have a very short time to live and I want to share with you a few of my heartfelt thoughts at this moment. . . . I truly feel that we were put on earth by God to love and help each other and help each other through this journey called life. . . . Please remember to love each other and help each other all of your lives on earth.

In his speech at the luncheon for Bo's Place, Secretary of State James Baker III, accustomed to negotiating intricate agreements around the world, talked about the necessity of others in this journey of life:

> The truth is, we can't do it alone because a life of faith often travels the road less traveled, and negotiating that road demands the guidance and support of friends. My spiritual journey, and yours, too, I am sure, is a story of friends and friendship, the lasting personal relationships that enrich our lives and help us find our way through the times of loss.

As we go through life, we must hold each other and hold each other up. We must bear with each other and bear each other's burdens in healthy ways. We must honor the losses and respect the sorrows that each human being carries, but we must be willing, as well, to say "Yes" to life.

We must be willing, when it is time, to let go of our suffering and embrace joy. We must be willing to choose life, day by day by day.

Why be good?

We are called to goodness for love's sake and because of love and because we have been loved.

Why do we serve God?

We serve God because he has loved us so much and he keeps on loving us. God loves each of us as if each of us is the only one he has, and God loves all of us the same, and what God wants from us is neither duty nor obligation, but love.

There are no answers that will satisfy a broken heart, but love can heal its wounds.

My friend Carmen LePere has cared for her husband Gerald since a terrible stroke ended his career as a campus minister at Rice University over twenty-five years ago. Gerald's stroke and subsequent disability was a devastating loss for Carmen and Gerald, and for their two young daughters, and each of them has suffered in different ways.

In 2001, Carmen and I were together in Seattle, Washington, at a retreat that preceded a choir tour of Canada with the choir of South Main Baptist Church of Houston. I was the retreat leader and Carmen, a choir member, called me into her room one day during our break.

Weeping, Carmen described her sorrow for Gerald and the heaviness of their situation, and my heart broke for her. The burden and care of life was so overwhelming for her, and in that moment, she needed to mourn her burden.

Carmen understands long term suffering and though, as she says it, she is "tired of being an icon" and a model of longsuffering, nevertheless, she has shown me and countless others how to sit strong over a long period of time. She shows us every day how to thrive in the face of suffering that lasts on and on.

In Seattle, Carmen had hit a low spot. Her words to me that day in Seattle and then, how she lives reminds me of the lines of Samuel Beckett: "I cannot go on. I will go on."

Day after day, Carmen cares for Gerald with uncommon grace and patience. She stays alive by staying involved with her church. She and I take classes at the Jung Center together. She travels and reads, sings with different choral groups and converses about sports and politics. Always, laughter is close to the surface, and she speaks with a wry wit.

If it is true, as Teilhard de Chardin says that "joy is the most infallible sign of the Presence of God," then God is deeply present in Carmen who lives with what she calls "on-going grief over a long period of time." Perhaps what I've learned from Carmen is that joy is often most beautiful when it is mingled with sorrow.

While I was teaching the Book of Job, Carmen told those in the Thursday Morning Bible Study about the making of fine porcelain pieces in Japan. Occasionally, a piece is broken, but instead of throwing the broken pieces away, they are put back together with gold or other precious metals. In that way, that which is flawed becomes even more beautiful and valuable because of its broken places, repaired with gold.

Some of the most beautiful parts of human beings are those places where they have been broken and been put back together with the gold of love, grace and mercy.

Even as she carries the pain her husband has endured and is boldly honest about her feelings in the midst of it all, Carmen has found ways to thrive in the face of her sorrows. Carmen has learned well that it is important not to waste our sorrows. Consistently she passes on the wisdom, the compassion, and the tenderness that is the gold in the broken places of her life.

I cannot explain why Gerald has had to suffer as he has, or why Carmen has had to bear this sorrow, but I do know that she models compassion and grace.

Week after week, Carmen is my teacher.

Others have taught me by their sorrows what it means to sit strong, and I have been tested on the ash heap of my own suffering.

Job is my teacher, and now, after all these years with him, I have come to say about Job what Michelangelo's biographer, Giorgio Vasari, said about him: "He was my friend, as all the world knows."

He is my friend who points me beyond my sorrow and my suffering to that Holy Friend who is with me always and, in all ways, granting me what I need to sit strong and, finally, bringing me out of darkness and into the Light.

It is God who brings joy, at last, and in God's presence, there is joy.

Yes. I say yes. Yes . . . to life!
Yes . . . to love!
    I choose you,
    Holy One.
        I accept the gift of choosing, and I choose life!

I say it now:
Yes!—to the fullness of life,
    to abundance,
    to the joys
    and the sorrows,
    the victories and the defeats.
        I choose life—all of it and all of its abundance.

Yes!—to loving you and loving others,
    to forgiving and being forgiven,
    to mercy and to grace,
    to labor and to rest,
    to pleasure and to pain,

to laughter and to tears,
to trouble and to trauma,
to calmness and to ecstasy.
    I accept it all.

Yes!—to the burdens and the blessings, to the gains and the losses.
Yes!—to uncertainty.
Yes!—to the unknown.
Yes!—to the imperfect, the incomplete, and the flawed.
Yes!—to the gains and successes.
Yes!—to the losses and the failures.
Yes!—to my life and your life, alive and at work in mine.
Yes!—to this present moment.
Yes!—to life!

Reading Job:
A Spiritual Exercise

Over my lifetime, I have found that turning to the basic spiritual practices of prayer and meditation, Bible study, spiritual reading and daily journaling has been invaluable in daily life, and especially in crisis. In a sense, the practices that I learned as a child, which I originally did to meet external standards, did give me what I needed to form a firm foundation of faith. Like Job, there came a time when I reached to God out of love instead of duty. I began to make these practices a part of my life not because I wanted to look good, but because they fed my soul and kept me centered..

The following questions may be used for reflection on the biblical story. At the end of the questions for the chapters of the biblical narrative are questions for personal reflection and journaling. May all of the questions lead you to a deeper encounter with the Living God and with your own soul. May your personal reflection be transforming and healing to you.

Before you begin the study of Job, you might want to respond to the following questions in a journal. After working through the following questions and reading this book, revisit these questions and see if your answer have changed.

1. What is your own personal sorrow that you would take to "the ash heap"?

2. Do you believe that te thing you think you cannot bear contains within it the possibility of redemption for you?

3. Would you even want to be transformed? What are you willing to do for God to help you?

4. Is there something in your life you are carrying in the secret places of your memory or your heart? What are the effects of keeping this secret?

5. Is there some unresolved problem that you need to face, a relationship issue that you need to acknowledge or a character defect you are avoiding? Are your creative energies being drained by what you are hiding?

6. What does it cost you to avoid facing the things you won't face?

7. Who do you know who is stronger, more compassionate and more tender-hearted because of the way he or she has "suffered" a personal tragedy?

8. Who do you know who is more bitter and is smaller because of the way he or she has suffered a personal tragedy? What is the difference in those who become bitter and those who are transformed by their suffering?

9. What do you need to give you the courage to own your own personal pain, analyze it and carry it in a new way?

10. Is what you are carrying your own pain, or did you inherit it?

11. Are you carrying someone else's pain to "protect" them, depriving them of the opportunity to grow up?

12. What is the payoff for staying stuck? What is the cost? Who's paying for it?

READ JOB 1

1. List the basic facts of Job's life. What does these tell you about this man?

2. What do you think it means to "fear God"?

3. What do you think it means that Job was "the greatest man among all of the people of the East?"

4. Describe Job's family life. Who was the religious leader of the family? What does this tell you about his family?

5. What do you make of the conversation between God, the angels and Satan? What is your reaction to this conversation?

6. What is meant by verse 12?

7. List the tragedies that befell Job. How do you think each one affected him?

8. Doesn't Job's reaction, described in verse 20, strike you as strange? What do you make of it?

9. Is Job's prayer in verse 21 fatalism or faith?

10. List all of the ways Job could have responded to his tragedy.

For Personal Reflection

11. What is your greatest fear today?

12. Other than that, what is your greatest fear?

13. List all of the ways you typically cope with difficulty. How effective are those ways?

14. What do you hope to gain from the study of the Book of Job?

15. How would you describe yourself? Are you a religious person? A good person? A spiritual person? How would God describe you?

16. In a crisis, will your "center" hold?

17. What do you think you need in order to strengthen your own courage and faith?

READ JOB 2

1. What is the most troubling thing about the conversations between God and Satan?

2. Why on earth, if God knows everything, did he ask Job if he "considered" his servant Job?

3. What do you think God's definition of "integrity" is?

4. Why does Satan want to attack Job's health?

5. Why did God allow Satan to do this heinous thing?

6. What do you make of the idea, in verse 7, that it was outside the presence of God that Satan did this deed? Where is that, outside the presence of God, if God is everywhere and in all things?

7. At this point, what was Mrs. Job thinking? feeling? wanting?

8. What would have happened if Job had, indeed, cursed God? What would that have accomplished?

9. How do you think Job's wife responded to Job's position, expressed in verse 10?

10. When the three friends were on their way to see Job, what do you think they expected to do and say when they got there?

11. When they reacted with weeping and tearing their robes, what were they feeling? How do you suppose their outward show of angst affected Job?

12. What is the meaning of their seven day silent sit-in?

For Personal Reflection

13. How do the first two chapters of Job affect you? Do you want to continue with this study?

14. How do the hard questions of life affect you? Do you want to address them, or do you prefer not to?

15. Which of these do you best, when confronted with something hard? Avoid it Explain it away Analyze it Deny it Euphemize it Minimize it Maximize it Anesthetize it Rationalize it Blame it away Put it off until later Cry Become helpless Get very organized

16. It has been said that some problems need "judicious neglect" and "the tincture of time." What do you think is meant by those terms? When might they be needed, and when do they become avoidance?

17. What is the hardest question or issue in your life right now? What do you think God's point of view is about this issue? What is your current anxiety management technique that you are applying to the problem? Is it working? What do you think you need to do about it?

READ JOB 3

1. What do you think it was that made Job finally speak?

2. Why do you think Job cursed the day of his birth? Why did he choose that response?

3. In which stage of grief was Job at this point? Denial Anger Bargaining Depression Acceptance

4. Would you say that Job's response was a natural response to what had happened to him?

5. What purpose do "why" questions serve?

6. Verse 25 is a significant verse in this chapter. What does it tell us about Job and what has motivated him?

7. How does what Job said in verse 25 throw new light and understanding on God's "willingness" to let him be tested?

8. In your view, what is the difference between being disciplined.....and being punished.....and being tested?

9. So—did Job truly "fear" God? Or was he looking after his own welfare and image? And if he was looking after himself, what does this say about his trust in God?

10. At this point, is Job's "center" (of faith) "holding"?

11. Job describes his emotional, psychological and spiritual state in verse 26. How does this compare with a contemporary person in trouble?

For Personal Reflection

12. Pick the greatest difficulties in your life. What are the "why" questions you have asked of God, of others, of yourself in these situations? Where have your "why" questions led you? If verse 25 reflects a set-up for a self-fulfilling prophecy, would you think It would be a good idea to give up fear? Do you know your greatest fear? How do you handle it?

READ JOB 4-7

1. In analyzing Chapter 4, what would you say Eliphaz was wanting to communicate to Job?

2. What questions did Job's suffering evoke in Eliphaz?

3. How does the tone change in Chapter 5? What is "wrong" with Eliphaz' speech to Job? What is wrong with giving a speech to a suffering person, anyway?

4. Chapters 6 and 7 contain the depth of Job's anguish. What do see as Job's most painful issue that he must confront?

5. Would you say that Eliphaz "failed" Job? Explain your response.

6. In Chapter 7, Job turns his anger toward God. What does the ability to do that say about Job's relationship with God?

7. At one point, it is as if Job "gives God notice", saying, "I am rising to the challenge you have placed before me." Where do you see that moment?

8. It has been said that only a person of faith dares to question God as Job did. Do you agree with this? If so, are there limits to the lengths one can go in questioning God?

9. Do you see evidence of Job's awareness of God's love in 7:17-21? Explain your response.

For Personal Reflection

10. When you are hurting, what do you want and need from your friends?

11. When your friend is hurting, what feelings does your friend's pain evoke in you? What do you do? What do you want to do?

12. What is your deepest fear? Are you able to bring that fear into consciousness, name it and surrender it to God? If not, why not?

13. What do you see as evidence of God's love in your own life? Can you see God's love in your difficulties or your hardest questions?

14. If you could ask God your most difficult question today, what would it be?

15. How do you feel when someone applies logic to your deepest pain?

16. How do you feel about others' knowing about your deepest pain?

17. What good are friends—even friends who don't know what to say or do —even friends who do the wrong thing and say the wrong thing— when you are in pain?

18. What do you most need from friendships at this point in your life?

19. What are you willing to do to get what you need from friends?

20. What are you willing to give to a friend who is hurting?

21. What obstacles stand in your way of getting/giving what you need?

READ JOB 8-10

1. If you had been Job, listening to the words of Bildad, recorded in Job 8:1-7, what would you have felt?

2. In verses 8-10, Bildad advises Job with "look backward" guidance. Indeed, there is much to be gained in looking back to the wisdom of the past. There is, however, a danger. What is the danger?

3. In verses 11-19, Bildad seems to be indulging in logical thinking. How comforting do you think that was to Job? Was he right in what he was saying? How was his timing?

4. In verses 20-22, Bildad seems to be looking forward. If you had been Job, do you think you would have felt encouraged by these words? Do you think Job thought Bildad knew what he was talking about? And do you think Job believed what Bildad said, at this point in his process?

5. In Chapter 9, Job seems to be getting in touch with the grandeur of God. In other words, his concept of God is exploding out of the box. If you agree with this, can you find evidence of it?

6. In Chapter 9, we see the foreshadowing of Christ, the Mediator. Where do you find this?

7. In Chapter 10, Job is moving toward a full acceptance of his plight. What is that plight? What changes do you sense in his process?

8. What feelings do you have about Job, at this point?

For Personal Reflection

9. When your old answers don't work any longer, how do you feel? When you can't fix another person with what has always worked before, or with what has worked for you, how do you feel?

10. When you feel shamed, what do you do?

11. Who is the hardest person for you to speak up to when times are hard?

12. What is it about blinding grief that makes a person see more clearly?

READ JOB 11-14

1. What would you say is the "feeling tone" of Zophar's speech to Job? How do you think his words must sound to Job, and how do you think Job must feel, hearing them?

2. What is it that makes Zophar speak with such authority about God to Job?

3. In Job 11:11, Zophar calls Job "deceitful". On what grounds do you think Zophar is making that judgment? What effect do you think it has on Job?

4. What is the "feeling tone" in Job's response to Zophar in Ch. 12?

5. Do you think that Job is feeling humbled or humiliated, at this point?

6. How do you feel about Job, reading his response to his friends?

7. From Job's response, what do you think is the most painful aspect of his situation to him? What do you think is the most painful thing to the friends?

8. In Job 13:3, Job lets the friends know that he needs and desires a higher authority than they. What does this tell you about his relationship with God?

9. What does Job's request to God in Job 13:20-32 tell you about Job's spiritual health?

10. Reread Chapters 11-14 and note the shifting feeling tones throughout. What does this reveal about the nature of suffering and the people who suffer?

11. It has been argued that Job, on the ash heap, manifests more vital faith in God than his friends do. Would you agree with this, and if so, why?

12. It has been said that "there is more faith in honest doubting than in untested certainty." Would you agree with that, and if so, why?

13. What evidence of anxiety do you see in the friends?

For Personal Reflection

14. If you had been Job, what would you have wanted to hear, given your circumstances?

15. What kinds of things do you say things to yourself that cause you to shame yourself?

16. What kinds of things do you say to scare yourself?

17. Why would a person torment herself with words that shame or scare? What possible payback could there be to doing that?

18. What does it take to stop the self-defeating self-talk?

READ JOB 15-17

1. It would appear that Eliphaz has "taken off the gloves" in Ch. 15, as the second round of discourses begins. What evidence of this do you find?

2. If you had been Job, listening to these words, would you feel shamed? Do you think it was Eliphaz' intent to shame Job? Explain your response.

3. In verses 20-35, Eliphaz speaks what is the conventional wisdom of his day. Do you agree with it? Do you think that what he is saying is consistent with the nature of God? Does he speak for God? Does that conventional wisdom apply today? Explain.

4. According to Eliphaz, what does it mean to be wicked? Does this description fit what we know of God? Why can't Eliphaz see the inconsistencies in his speech? Does this speech really belong to Job? Is it really for him?

5. What is it in Job that frees him to speak so boldly to his friends, as he does in Ch. 16?

6. What does Job say he would do if the roles were reversed?

7. The anguish in Job seems to deepen in 16:6-17. Why do you think this is?

8. Why might the state Job is in, as expressed in 16:18-17:2 be seen as progression in his grief process?

9. It appears in 17:4-5 that Job has a clearer grasp of what is going on than his friends. How can that be possible?

10. The words of Job reveal a man whose heart has been broken open. Why is this a good thing?

For Personal Reflection

11. Do you have someone in your life who specializes in bringing your self-image and self-esteem down? How do you handle this person?

12. Are YOU that person to someone else? What do you get out of being that kind of "friend"?

13. Can you find any situation in which Jesus shamed someone?

READ JOB 18

1. Can you make the defense that this speech of Bildad's was the "speech of common sense"?

2. Do you think Bildad was defensive or sincere?

3. Do you think he was self-righteous? Was he justified in what he said?

4. What do you think his intent was? Was he trying to shame Job or to strike terror in him? Do you think he thought he was helping?

5. Can you find any false logic in Bildad's speech? Explain.

6. Why would the punishment described in verses 19-20 be the ultimate punishment for a man of Job's day and belief system?

7. Do you see grandiosity in verses 19-20? Explain.

8. Put yourself in Job's shoes, as much as you can. How would these words have sounded to you? What would you have felt if they had been directed at you?

9. What can you find within this speech that would be helpful?

For Personal Reflection

10. Have you ever felt that "dark grandiosity", when it feels like you have the "best, worst problem of all? — that your suffering is the worst of all? What was that like for you? How did you move through it? Or, did you?

12. What is a helpful response to someone who is caught in dark grandiosity?

13. What is the problem with "staying with" dark grandiosity?

READ JOB 19

1. Would you say that Job is "being born again", or that he is trying to "give birth" to something?

2. If you could say that "something" is being born in the heart of Job, what might that be?

3. If this is Job's "dark night of the soul", what qualities make it that?

4. What is Job's relationship to God like at this point?

5. Why do you think God and all of his mighty forces would "need" to surround one tent with one man in it? (vs. 12) Could this be a bit of "dark grandiosity"?

6. Judging from this chapter, what kind of support is job getting from family and the rest of his friends? What must this be like for him?

7. Is it possible that Job is overstating others' reactions? Could they just be busy with their own issues, or consumed with their own lives?

8. Where is the breakthrough moment in this chapter, the words that indicate a Light in the darkness?

9. Do you think Job even realizes that the breakthrough has occurred?

10. If you were to restate in your own words the desire of Job's heart, as he expressed it in vs. 27b, how would you say it?

11. What on earth does Job mean by his "warning" in vss. 28-29? Is his warning valid?

12. At this point, what do you think Job wanted and/or needed from his friends? Did he get what he really needed, even though it seemed so harsh?

For Personal Reflection

13. What is your preferred defense when you hear something you don't want to hear?

14. What does it cost a person to "let in" new information or insight about God? What is required for a person to tolerate a different point of view about God? What happens if you don't open your mind to new points of view?

15. How can you know if you've been so close-minded that God cannot get through to you?

16. How can you know if you have been so "open-minded that your brains fall out"?

READ JOB 20-21

1. Why, after Job's words in Job 19:20-26, would the friends have any need of saying anything else?

2. In looking at Zophar's speech, do you find any indication that he has heard what Job has said?

3. What was it in Zophar that made him incapable of "getting it"? What are his defenses and his anxiety management techniques?

4. Zophar says "my thoughts answer me," and "because of my haste within me." He says, "out of my understanding a spirit answer me". What is wrong with these statements, if anything?

5. Is what Zophar says in this chapter true? Is it relevant? Are words that are true helpful if they are not relevant?

6. Would you say that Zophar is expressing more anxiety and insecurity than the other two friends? If so, why would he be doing that? If not, what is he expressing?

7. Job seems to be speaking with a new level of calmness and serenity. Where is that coming from? How is it possible? Has anything changed externally?

8. If you were one of the friends, how would you answer Job's question in vss. 15-16?

9. What did it take for Job to speak the words in Vs. 34 to his friends?

10. What has shifted within Job, as revealed in this chapter?

For Personal Reflection

11. When things are tough and you feel as if you are on an emotional roller-coaster, what behaviors help keep you stabilized and which behaviors make things worse?.

12. When you are in emotional and spiritual pain, what can you do to manage the pain and harvest the gold from the pain without numbing the pain? In other words, how can you cooperate with the pain and tolerate it at the same time?

13. In the face of the reality of "man's inhumanity to man", and God's seeming unwillingness to intervene when and how we think God should or could, what is a person to do?

READ JOB 22

1. From this third discourse of Eliphaz', what would you say his (Eliphaz') mood is by now?

2. Would you say that, so far, the friends have failed in their set purpose? Why or why not?

3. Is God affected by our spiritual state? Our emotional health? Our well-being? How does God feel about us, anyway?

4. It has been said that "every man's god is a reflection of himself." What does this mean? How does it apply to the words of Eliphaz to Job?

5. Stories spread when a person is down like Job is. What would you say of vss. 6-11? What are the facts? What is the rumor?

6. How is Eliphaz' concept of God limited and limiting? How does his concept of God box Job in? How do we affect each other for the ill? For the good?

7. It has been said that exhortation is notoriously futile. If you were Job, listening to the exhortation in vss. 21-30, would you have been able to make the changes necessary to get yourself out of your anguish?

8. Is there anything Eliphaz could have said that really would have made a Difference? Is there any time that exhortation works?

9. Eliphaz speaks wisdom, however, in vs. 21: "Acquaint yourself with God...." How could this make a difference in Job's experience? But whatdoes Eliphaz mean by it?

For Personal Reflection

10. Where are you stuck in your own spiritual journey at the beginning? Is it possible that your stuckness is a reflection of a limited and limiting understanding of God, of yourself, or of your own personal burden that you have been called to suffer?

11. If an answer to suffering might be "acquainting ourselves with God", what might this mean for you? Do you feel as if you've done all the work and God is still in hiding, keeping you on hold or has gone on vacation?

12. What do you most need from God during this week? Is that what God would say that you need?

READ JOB 23-24

1. What is Job's complaint against God at this point in the process?

2. Would you say that Job's complaint is valid?

3. If you could translate Job 23:3-9 into your language, out of your own personal situation, what would you say?

4. Job perceives God as hiding from him. He perceives himself as being unable to find him, and if he should find him, unable to connect with him. What is the truth here?

5. There is a shift in verse 10. What is the shift? (from what to what?) What do you think caused the shift? Is it a shift in perception or in reality?

6. What does Job mean that he will "come forth as gold", in verse 10?

7. Job seems to be describing his faithfulness in verses 11 and 12. Is this confidence or blindness, the truth or self-promotion?

8. What is the source of job's assurance in verse 14? Is it justified?

9. Why does he shift back to terror in verses 15-17? Why can't this guy get on solid ground?

10. In Chapter 24, Job seems to be describing "man's inhumanity to man" and God's seeming lack of interest in intervening. Does it seem to you that he is agreeing with the things that Eliphaz has said. Explain.

For Personal Reflection

9. What do those who have truly suffered have to teach us about God?

10. If it is in the suffering that we experience the depth of God's grace, love and mercy, why do we resist our suffering so much?

11. When have you been taught by someone you thought you were teaching?

12. If someone were to ask you today what you know about "the hand of God", (27:11), what would you say? Would your words come from a classroom discussion, or from your own life experience?

13. What do you know about God's mercy, from your own life?

READ JOB 25-27

1. Some commentators suggest that Bildad is, in this speech, running out of steam. Others take the opposite view and suggest that he reaches a new level of self-righteousness as he highlights Job's "arrogance." What is your take on this short passage? What would the body language of Bildad be? What do you think his tone of voice would be?

2. Abraham Lincoln once said, "Oh, why should the spirit of mortal be proud?" What is your definition of pride? What is "healthy" pride? What is "afflictive" pride? Where does Job fall, in the "pride" issue?

3. What is the tone of Job's words in 26:1-4?

4. If it is as it seems, and Job's words are blistering sarcasm, what is going on with Job, at this point? How dare a man in his situation resort to such sarcasm, for crying out loud?

5. Who is having a harder time grasping the idea of the power of God, Job or Bildad?

6. Job reaffirms his innocence in 27:1-12. Where does he get the strength to do this?

7. By this time, the three friends must be at their wit's end. What hope do you see for them, if any?

8. The tables have definitely turned in 27:11. Can you even imagine that it is Job who is going to teach the friends who are full of answers about God? What do you think their response is, at this boldness of Job's?

For Personal Reflection

11. What positive purpose does a review of the past serve?

12. How is it helpful to take a look at your motivations in the past with the eyes of today's understanding and knowledge?

13. When you review your life, how do you justify the things you did in the past? Does justifying help you move forward? Does it help you gain perspective in the present? Does it keep you stuck, repeating the same patterns? Could there be some other way to view the past instead of justifying?

14. In what part of your life do you need to apply grace and say, "I did what I did because at the time and with the knowledge I had at the time, I thought it was the right thing to do"?

READ JOB 28-29

1. When you read Job 28:1-11, do you want to ask, "And so, Job, what is your point?" What do you think his point is, anyway? Do you agree with him?

2. Job 28:12-21 has been called "one of the most impressive bits of poetry in literature. What about this passage would earn it this accolade?

3. What is Job's point in verses 12-21? Do you agree with him?

4. If only God knows the way to wisdom, as Job seems to indicate in 28:22-28, is it futile for us to see it?

5. Does God want us to have wisdom or have a relationship with him more?

6. In verses 22-28, Job seems to set the context for wisdom in nature. What do you make of this?

7. In verse 28, Job says, "the fear of the Lord – that is wisdom." How can you incorporate that truth with the teachings and spirit of Jesus?

8. Job regresses somewhat in Chapter 29. What evidence of this do you see? What purpose does regression serve, ultimately?

9. In Job 29:14-20, Job reviews his righteousness. What purpose does this serve?

10. Is Job's review of his righteousness an act of his ego or of his True Self?

For Personal Reflection

11. What are your most well-loved and well-used defenses in life?*

12. What purpose do your defenses serve?

13. If someone young and fresh were to evaluate your life, what would she/he say about you?

14. Who is God to you? Who are you to God? Has either perspective changed since you started the study of Job?

15. Have you ever done a "fearless, searching moral inventory"? Would you like to do that? * remember.....if you say you don't have any defenses, that is, itself, a defense!

READ JOB 30-31

1. In Chapter 30, Job is wallowing in the "agony of the present." What are his current complaints?

2. Job is experiencing the agony of his existential angst, a loneliness too great to bear, and that loneliness is in sharp contrast to his earlier life. Can this part of his process serve any useful purpose? If so, what?

3. What does God's seeming absence feel like to Job?

4. What is that feeling of God's absence so terrible? Is it harder for those who have known his presence and then lost that knowing? Explain.

5. In Job 31, it is as if Job does a "fearless, searching moral inventory," similar to what is asked for in the Fourth Step of the Twelve Steps of Alcoholics Anonymous. What good does a moral inventory do?

6. What are the areas of life that Job inventories?

7. Would you say that Job has done a pretty good job of looking at himself, or does he still have areas of blindness?

8. If you were listening to Job's words in Chapter 31, as if they were a Fifth Step confession, what would your response be? How would you assess his sincerity? His humility? Was he hard on himself? Hard enough? Did he cut himself too much slack?

For Personal Reflection

9. At this point, it would be helpful to ask yourself the questions often asked in spiritual direction: Who am I to God? Who is God to me? How do you think Job would answer these questions, based on Chapters 30 and 31?

10. What is particularly painful about having young men mock him?

11. Do you think that Job has hit bottom? If so, what evidence do you have of that? When have you hit bottom? What was it like for you? What did God do at that time?

12. Do you think that Chapters 30 and 31 resemble a "searching, fearless moral inventory"? (a Fourth Step, in recovery programs) Or, is this another exercise in self-justification? Have you ever done this kind of inventory?

13. Chapters 30-31 have been called "the covenant of Job's innocence". Does that ring true with you? Explain your response. Have you ever had to plead your innocence? What was that like?

14. How does Job 32:1 strike you, especially the phrase, "because he was righteous in his own eyes"?

15. So, what do you think of the young Elihu?

16. What purpose does Elihu serve in this whole process?

17. If an inventory assesses both strength and weaknesses, assets and liabilities, what would your inventory include?

18. Have you ever made a confession to another human being? Would you like to do that?

READ JOB 32-33

1. Job 32:1 represents a major turning point in Job's story. What is happening that makes it so important?

2. What do you make of Elihu? What purpose does he serve in this process?

3. What evidence does Elihu give that he is a good listener? Is he?

4. What evidence does Elihu give that he understands the deeper mysteries of God better than the three older friends do?

5. Do you think Elihu is taking the side of the three friends to vindicate God, or is he playing the devil's advocate?

6. Do you se any evidence of humility in Elihu? Explain.

7. Is Elihu mellowed with love?

8. What evidence to you find to support the truth that man cannot make God in his own image in this story?

9. Does Elihu indicate that God speaks in the midst of pain? If so, where?

10. Do you think that Elihu is proposing that pain is an advanced level of communication with God? Explain.

11. What evidence to you find that Elihu proposes that God and the activity of God cannot be judged by human standards?

12. Is it possible that Elihu plays a "compensatory function" in the process, balancing the world view of the three friends? If so, explain.

13. How do you think Job reacted to Elihu?

For Personal Reflection

14. How do the young play a compensatory function within a family or a church?

15. How do these words apply to Job? Why are they important? "Wait a year before you judge a situation." "You can't know the outcome of the game at halftime."

16. Who is most likely to question your motives? How do you feel about that person?

17. What is important about questioning our own motives?

18. What "young" part of you is trying to get you to "move on" with your life?

19. What is your hardest unanswered question at this point in your life?

READ JOB 34-35

1. From the first four verses of Chapter 32, it seems that Elihu is no longer "speaking for God". Do you agree? Explain.

2. If is it accurate that Elihu's tone has shifted, how do you account for that?

3 Are Elihu's charges Job 34:5-9 accurate? Does he quote Job correctly?

4. What is Elihu's image of God?

5. Why does Elihu insult Job? What purpose does that serve? (34:34-37)

6. What right does Elihu have to question Job's motives? (35:1-8)

7. What is the single most important question that Elihu is bringing to the forefront of the drama?

8. What purpose does Elihu serve in creating the climate in which Job will hear God?

9. What do you *feel* about what Elihu is saying to Job?

10. If you were standing there with Job, listening to this long speech of Elihu's, what would you be feeling toward Job?

11. If you were one of the three friends, how would you feel about Elihu?

12. Do you see any hope whatsoever for Job at this point?

For Personal Reflection

13. Why is it important to ask ourselves the hard questions about life? What hard questions do you think God would ask you today? What hard questions are you avoiding?

14. What purpose does it serve for us to question our own motives? Where are your motives "less than pure"? Where are your motives mixed?

15. What is a good way to handle the questions that don't seem to have any immediate resolution or answer?

16. What do you need to do to make peace with your unresolved and unanswered questions?

17. What do most people do to distract themselves from the hard questions?

18. What is your hardest, unanswered question right now?

READ JOB 36-37

1. What do you think? Is Elihu arrogant, speaking for God as he does, or is he authentic?

2. Is Elihu creating the climate in which Job can hear God clearly, or is Elihu setting up barriers between God and Job?

3. What do you think the 3 friends are doing while Elihu goes on and on?

4. From reading Job 36:5-14, what would you say are the worst chains that bind a person?

5. In Job 36:15-16, we find the "key" to life's difficulties. What is it? (Hint: bear in mind the "philosophy of suffering" that has guided our study.)

6. In Job 36:17-21, Elihu delivers a strong warning to those who have been made vulnerable by their difficulties. What dangers and seductions entice contemporary persons who are in trouble?

7. Elihu brings Job back to his main point in verses 22-33. What is that point?

8. It has been said that contemporary persons long to know someone who has had a direct experience of the Living God. What evidence do you see that Elihu has had this experience in Chapter 37?

9. How do you feel about Elihu now?

10. How can you know when it is really God speaking?

11. If you had been Job, how would you have responded to what Elihu was saying? How would you have felt about his words?

For Personal Reflection

13. Has someone younger than you ever spoken truth to you, cutting through your defenses in a way that set you free to see your life or a situation in a new way?

14. Where in our culture does youth see more clearly than age?

15. How do we balance the new wisdom of youth with the experience of the old?

16. How can churches attract, accommodate and "keep" the young, while also honoring and serving older people?

READ JOB 38

1. Finally, The Lord speaks. What took him so long?

2. What does it mean that the Lord spoke "out of the storm"?

3. What does this passage tell us about God?

4. What is the point of all of God's questions to Job?

5. What does God tell us about himself in this chapter?

6. What does God tell us about humankind in this chapter?

7. What does God tell us about the relationship of God and persons in this chapter?

8. What does God tell us about creation in this chapter?

9. What do you think Job's response was to these questions?

10. What do you think? Is God speaking from the heavens, in a booming voice? Is God speaking in a whisper, sitting near Job? Was the voice audible? Is God speaking from within the heart and mind of Job? Did the friends hear the voice of God, or was Job the only one to hear him?

For Personal Reflection

11. In suffering, is it ours to question God, or is the real questioning coming from God to us? Explain your response.

12. What do you know about God now that you didn't know before this study?

13. What do you know about suffering that you didn't know before?

14. What do you know about yourself that you didn't know before?

15. Where do you think God will take you on your journey now? How much choice do you think you have about where that next part of your journey will take you?

16. Wise people "don't waste their sorrows." What does that mean for you?

READ JOB 39

1. What is God doing, talking about nature like he does?

2. What is God teaching Job?

3. What does God say about the way things work in the world?

4. What does God say about freedom and instinctual life?

5. What does God want us to know about his nature?

For Personal Reflection

6. Where do you see God's activity most clearly?

7. Where do you not think to look for God?

8. When do you experience the presence of God most?

9. What does God want to say to you about your True Self? About your instinctual life?

10. What is the point of looking for God, anyway?

11. What is your current big argument with God, if you have one?

12. If God were to speak to you right now, what approach would he use to get your attention? What would God say to you today?

13. What is God asking of you at this point in your life?

14. How does God want you to feel in your relationship with him? How do you feel?

READ JOB 40

1. Now, God is challenging Job. What do you think Job is thinking? What do you think he is doing? What is he feeling?

2. What do you think God wants from Job at this point?

3. How do you interpret Job's response to God in verses 4-5?

4. Is there a shift in Job's attitude? If so, what is it?

5. What is God really asking of Job at this point? What is he asking him?

6. A behemoth is a hippopotamus. Why would God use that animal to make a point with Job? What point is he making?

7. Do you see playfulness at all in God's response to Job? If so, why would be feeling playful?

For Personal Reflection

8. Does God ever appear to you in the form of "The Trickster"? Does God ever "play" with you?

9. What questions about your own life with God does God's speech to Job raise for you?

10. What shifts in understanding about the nature of life, of suffering, of God and of yourself have you had as a result of this study?

11. What unanswered questions do you still have about life?

READ JOB 41

1. If the leviathan is a symbol for evil that exists in opposition to the activity of God, what point is God making with his question to Job?

2. What is God saying in verse 9? What are the implications of this?

3. Read Matthew 13:24-30. How does Jesus' parable correlate with this passage in Job?

4. What does verse 11 reveal about God's relationship with evil?

5. In verses 12-33, God vividly describes the nature of evil. If you were writing this in contemporary language, what would you say about evil?

6. Read 1 Peter 5:8. How does this idea about evil correlate with the Job passage?

7. What are the implications of verses 33-34 for contemporary persons?

For Personal Reflection

8. How do you deal with the reality of evil in your own life?

9. What is your biggest faith challenge?

10. What are the ways you have in place of dealing with your own suffering? Your character defect? Your personal sin?

11. A notorious "sinner" once said on national television, "I do not trust anyone who hasn't suffered." What do you think he meant? Do you agree? Explain your response.

READ JOB 42

1. How has Job changed as a result of his suffering?

2. Do you think he has been transformed? Has he been healed? What evidence do you have of that?

3. How do you feel about Job's restoration, as described in the Epilogue?

For Personal Reflection

4. In what ways has your deepest suffering changed you?

5. How has God healed you?

6. In what ways are you resisting God's initiative of grace and mercy

7. At what price have you been transformed?

8. What have you lost, as a result of your suffering? What have you gained?

9. What do you think about God now?

10. If we are called to be good stewards of our own personal pain and suffering, what does that mean? How are you doing as a steward of your suffering?

11. What expectations of God have you had that God has not met?

12. What do you think God expects of you? Have you met God's expectations